Not only so, but we also glory in our sufferings, because we know that suffering produces perseverance; perseverance, character; and character, hope. And hope does not put us to shame, because God's love has been poured out into our hearts through the Holy Spirit, who has been given to us.

—Romans 5:3–5 (NIV)

MYSTERIES *of* BLACKBERRY VALLEY

Where There's Smoke
The Key Question
Seeds of Suspicion
A Likely Story
Out of the Depths
Run for the Roses
Crooks and Christmas Cookies

MYSTERIES of BLACKBERRY VALLEY

Crooks and Christmas Cookies

STEPHANIE COLEMAN

Guideposts

A Gift from Guideposts

Thank you for your purchase! We want to express our gratitude for your support with a special gift just for you.

Dive into *Spirit Lifters*, a complimentary e-book that will fortify your faith, offering solace during challenging moments. Its 31 carefully selected scripture verses will soothe and uplift your soul.

Please use the QR code or go to **guideposts.org/ spiritlifters** to download.

Mysteries of Blackberry Valley is a trademark of Guideposts.

Published by Guideposts
100 Reserve Road, Suite E200
Danbury, CT 06810
Guideposts.org

Copyright © 2025 by Guideposts. All rights reserved. This book, or parts thereof, may not be reproduced, stored in a retrieval system, or transmitted in any form or by any means, electronic, mechanical, photocopying, recording, or otherwise, without the written permission of the publisher.

This is a work of fiction. Apart from actual historical people and events that may figure into the fiction narrative, all other names, characters, businesses, and events are the creation of the author's imagination and any resemblance to actual persons, living or dead, or events is coincidental. Every attempt has been made to credit the sources of copyrighted material used in this book. If any such acknowledgment has been inadvertently omitted or miscredited, receipt of such information would be appreciated.

Scripture references are from the following sources: *The Holy Bible, King James Version* (KJV). *The Holy Bible, New International Version* (NIV). Copyright © 1973, 1978, 1984, 2011 by Biblica, Inc. Used by permission of Zondervan. All rights reserved worldwide. www.zondervan.com.

Cover and interior design by Müllerhaus
Cover illustration by Bob Kayganich at Illustration Online LLC.
Typeset by Aptara, Inc.

ISBN 978-1-965859-20-9 (hardcover)
ISBN 978-1-965859-21-6 (softcover)
ISBN 978-1-965859-22-3 (epub)

Printed and bound in the United States of America
10 9 8 7 6 5 4 3 2 1

Crooks and Christmas Cookies

Chapter One

Hannah Prentiss was already five minutes late for her meeting with Amelia Jacobsen, and she hadn't even left her restaurant yet. But as she hurried to the door, head chef Jacob Forrest flagged her down.

"I watched an online video on dry-aging meat," he said, his eyes alight with excitement. "It looks time-consuming but not hard."

"I would love to hear more about this later." Hannah took another step toward the dining room of the Hot Spot. "Can we talk when I get back?"

By then maybe she would have thought of a way to break it to him that they'd probably have to charge more for dry-aged meat than the people of Blackberry Valley would want to pay. Jacob was endlessly creative with food but often oblivious to the realities of the food budget.

As Hannah swept past the hostess stand, Elaine Wilby frowned at her. "I thought your meeting was at three."

"Think I'll be on time?" Hannah quipped. "Call if you need me."

Inside her car, Hannah took the time to send Amelia a quick text. SORRY I'M LATE! I SHOULD BE THERE IN FIVE MINUTES. What had she been thinking when she arranged this meeting for a Friday afternoon, one of her busiest times of the week?

She tucked her phone into her purse before pulling away from her usual parking spot outside the restaurant. When she saw one of the Holt twins had their patrol car parked outside Blackberry Market, she was grateful that she hadn't tried to speed on the way to Sally's Bed and Breakfast.

Or what would be Sally's Bed and Breakfast when it opened.

When Hannah first met Amelia a few months ago, Amelia had just moved to Blackberry Valley to help take care of her mother, Sally, who had owned a house on the edge of town for several years, a big place brimming with Southern charm. Hannah had never been inside, but she'd always admired its wide wraparound porch and the ornate trim work that rarely appeared in newly constructed homes.

For years, Sally had wanted to turn her childhood home into a bed and breakfast where she could serve guests all the foods that she was famous for among her friends. But Sally's husband had passed away not long after they purchased the property. Losing him so suddenly had aged Sally faster than anyone anticipated, and Amelia had moved in to help.

Like everyone else, Hannah had expected that Sally's death would lead to the big house going back on the market, but instead Amelia had fallen in love with the town and wanted to see her mother's dream come to fruition. While Amelia was older than Hannah's mother had been when she died, she reminded Hannah strongly of Frieda Prentiss. Hannah's mom had fought with grace until the end of her battle with cancer, and Amelia struck Hannah as the kind of woman with that same quiet strength. It would serve her well in her business endeavor.

Today, Hannah was meeting with Amelia to go over her menus and make suggestions before final orders were placed. Amelia, much like Jacob, had strong ideas about how the food at Sally's should look and taste but didn't yet know how to factor in the cost of ingredients or design a menu that eliminated food waste or stayed within budget.

A new sign had been put near the end of the drive. SALLY'S, it read in a tasteful, loopy font. The circular drive held two trucks and a work van. Converting the house to a bed and breakfast was a big job, and it looked like everyone was on task today. Hannah parked alongside a shiny Jeep Cherokee that seemed out of place then grabbed her purse and rushed up the steps of the wrap-around porch.

She knocked on the door. Inside were sounds of drilling and hammering, so it was probably okay to simply walk inside, but it still felt strange.

"Are you here to see Amelia?" asked a male voice from behind her.

Hannah turned and found herself sharing the porch with Isaac Jacobsen, Amelia's nephew. Isaac was from Nashville, and Hannah always felt awkward and unpolished in his presence. He was about her age, maybe a couple of years younger, and wore his clothes more tailored, his hair sleeker, and his shoes shinier than other men she knew in town.

"Yes, I am," Hannah said with a smile. "I'm afraid I'm a bit late."

"Come on in." Isaac pushed the door open, and the cacophony of construction noises became even louder. "Your name is Hannah, right? You own the Hot Spot?" He grinned, showcasing a mouthful of gleaming white teeth. "I had an excellent dinner there several nights ago. Fried smoked chicken, mashed potatoes, and roasted vegetables." He formed a chef's kiss with his fingers. "Amazing."

Hannah swelled with pride. "All locally sourced too. Our eggs come from my best friend, Lacy's, chickens, and they're incredible. And most of our vegetables are from—"

"No, you listen to me!" screeched a female voice.

"Excuse me," Isaac murmured. He headed toward the sound.

Hannah lingered in the entry, feeling increasingly uncomfortable as every loud word reached her ears.

"I have lost everything because of you and your stupid delays!" The same woman continued to rant. "I should've been getting married tomorrow, and now I'm not, and it's all because of you!"

Hannah heard the low timbre of Isaac's voice as he entered the conversation, but she couldn't make out his actual words.

"I've had enough of your fake apologies," the woman snapped. "This isn't over. I will make you pay for what you did to me!"

Seconds later, the woman appeared in the hallway. Considering how loud she'd been, she was much smaller and younger than Hannah had anticipated. She appeared to be in her twenties, maybe even right out of college. She couldn't have been more than five feet tall, with beautiful dark hair that fell to her shoulders, a striking olive complexion, and cheekbones like a runway model's.

The woman's dark eyes landed on Hannah. "Whatever you do, do not trust either of them." Her voice was low and hot with anger. She jabbed a finger in the direction she'd come from. "They're liars."

With that, the woman marched to the front door, flung it open, and slammed it shut behind her. She stormed across the patio and stomped to the Jeep Cherokee.

Upstairs, a drill whirred, drawing Hannah back to the activity inside the house. Once again, she could hear the low rumble of

Isaac's voice, only this time she could also hear the soft sounds of someone crying. Probably Amelia.

Feeling like an intruder, Hannah ventured several steps down the hall. "Amelia?" she called tentatively.

But it was Isaac who answered, "Come on back, Hannah. We're in the kitchen."

Hannah followed the hall around a bend and stepped into a huge kitchen that took her breath away. Renovations were complete in here, apparently.

Isaac gave her a tight smile. "My aunt has gone to the restroom to wash her face and collect herself. I'm sorry you had to hear that."

"I'm sorry it happened," Hannah said. "Would it be better for me to come another time?"

"No, now's fine." Isaac waved away her suggestion. "Aunt Amelia will be back in a moment. Coffee?"

"Sure. Thank you."

Hannah's hand rested on the cool, quartz countertop, and she took in the splendor of the kitchen. The professional range, the stainless-steel prep area, the espresso machine, the enormous refrigerator. She'd been in many impressive kitchens over the course of her career, but not many brand-new ones. Hannah felt an irrational desire to move in.

A pocket door slid open, and Amelia stepped out. "Sorry to keep you waiting, Hannah," she said in her soft voice. Her face was blotchy, and her eyes were red.

"No apology necessary. I'm sorry for your trouble." Hannah smiled at Isaac as he handed her a mug of coffee. "Thank you. This smells divine."

He grinned at her. "Coffee is kind of my thing."

His grin looked strange alongside Amelia's frown.

Amelia took in a shuddering breath. "Violet is understandably angry with me. She was supposed to have her wedding ceremony here tomorrow, but that was before the whole…incident with my first contractor. When everything got delayed, we tried to make different arrangements with Violet, but it didn't go well."

Isaac snorted. "That's putting it mildly. Violet took the news so poorly that her husband-to-be got spooked and called the whole thing off."

While Isaac seemed unfazed by Violet's visit, Amelia looked as though she might burst into tears again.

"I feel terrible about what happened." Amelia took a towel from its hook and wiped the kitchen faucet, which already appeared to be perfectly clean. "I refunded her deposit. I offered to find a different date of her choosing at no cost. I tried to get her booked at Blackberry Inn, but Sabrina didn't have the availability."

Hannah wasn't too surprised that Amelia had gone to such lengths to make the situation right, and it only made her more upset that Violet had been so unpleasant to Amelia.

"You did your best," Isaac said as Amelia scrubbed the already-clean counter. "Let it go."

He wasn't being unkind, exactly, but he was behaving as though his aunt was overreacting. Hannah had been shouted at more than a few times in her line of work—such was life in the restaurant business—and more than once had cried afterward. Being told to "let it go" was never helpful.

"It sounds like you did everything you could," Hannah said, making her voice as warm as possible. "And you certainly can't help that her fiancé broke off the engagement when he saw how she reacted."

"I suppose not." Amelia bit her lower lip. "She'll probably say horrid things to all her friends though. This won't be good for business, and we're not even open yet."

"Does she live in town?" Hannah asked, after sipping her coffee. "I didn't recognize her."

"No," Amelia said. "Cave City, I think."

"I don't think we need to worry about her." Isaac handed a steaming mug of coffee to his aunt. "Sure, she might say some bad things to friends, but she strikes me as the type who's overly critical. People will probably shrug it off as Violet being Violet."

"Maybe," Amelia murmured.

"And as soon as people taste Grandma's legendary rosemary lemon shortbread, they really won't care what Violet's saying," he added.

This coaxed the slightest smile onto Amelia's face, so Hannah chimed in, "Absolutely. I would drive clear to Louisville for Sally's shortbread. Or a piece of her chocolate tart."

Amelia's face brightened considerably.

"I assume you know not to bother asking for the recipes," Isaac said with a grin.

"Oh, I know." Hannah returned the smile. "We've all tried. 'Family secrets.'"

"More like Grandma-and-Aunt-Amelia secrets." Isaac leaned against the counter and sipped from his own cup. "I'm family, and

I'm still not privy to the recipes. Maybe we should call this place 'Secret Sally's.'"

Amelia glanced at the clock and yelped. "How is it almost three thirty already? I'm sorry I've kept you waiting so long, Hannah. Don't you open soon?"

Hannah waved away Amelia's concerns. "No need to apologize. My team can handle opening if needed. Do you feel like going over your menus, or would you rather hold off?"

"Let's do it now. With our estimated opening in less than three weeks, I really can't afford to put it off any longer." Amelia gestured to an area that would normally hold a small kitchen table but contained a desk instead. A tin of candy was open on it. "Would you like some toffee?" she asked.

Hannah eagerly reached for a square. "You don't have to ask me twice."

Sally's desserts were legendary in these parts. She had been known for her rough, abrupt manner, but the more time Hannah had spent with her, the more she'd liked her. She'd been sad to hear of Sally's death.

While interacting with Sally was an acquired taste, her baked goods were not. Unlike most women, Sally had refused to share her recipes, saying they were her intellectual property and would someday draw throngs of visitors to Blackberry Valley.

Hannah hummed as the candy melted on her tongue. Sally's toffees were the perfect blend of buttery, salty, and sweet. How many pieces would a polite woman take? And how much value did Hannah place on being viewed as a polite woman?

"I just wonder what she'll do now," Amelia said as she settled behind her desk. The regret and sorrow in her tone signaled to Hannah that the conversation had returned to the bitter bride.

"I think you handled it well, given the circumstances," Hannah insisted. "You even called Blackberry Inn, offering your competition the business to make it right with her. That's above and beyond."

Amelia nodded slowly. "Yes, but I don't think Violet Presley sees it that way." She sighed. "I don't know what she'll do or say, of course, but I can feel in my bones that what happened with Violet will come back to haunt me somehow."

Hannah didn't want to say it aloud, but recalling the fire in Violet's eyes as she'd stormed out the front door, she had to agree.

Chapter Two

Hannah watched Lacy Minyard scatter chicken feed across the yard with an expert hand, as she imagined previous generations of Lacy's family had done over the last few decades.

Lacy grabbed another fistful of feed. "All I'm saying is that both you and Liam had a good time on your date. I think you should say something to him."

A cold December wind whipped across Lacy's farm, and Hannah pulled her hat lower over her ears. "Like what? At the end of the night, he said he would call me about the next one."

"And what did you say?"

"Well." Hannah squinted up at the sky, trying to recall the end of her one and only official date with Fire Chief Liam Berthold. "I don't remember exactly, but I responded favorably. I know that for sure."

Lacy blinked at Hannah, her hazel eyes expressing both compassion and exasperation all at once. "Hannah, that was *weeks* ago."

Hannah poked the cold ground with the toe of her sneaker. "I know."

"Don't you think Liam might need a little additional encouragement?"

Hannah crossed her arms over her chest. "When he ate at the Hot Spot last night, I gave him an extra scoop of ice cream with his pie."

It had been her waitress, Raquel Holden's, idea, and Hannah had used it because Raquel had won over Marshall Fredericks, a local food critic, with a similar technique. These days, they looked really happy together. And a little extra ice cream certainly couldn't hurt.

"I apologize for my suggestion then," Lacy said, turning her smirk toward the chickens. "I had no idea you were already communicating so clearly with Liam."

Hannah attempted to scowl at her best friend, but Lacy's grin made it clear that she'd failed. "I don't want to seem too forceful. He said he would call me."

Lacy frowned. "Expressing interest in another date isn't forceful."

"But maybe he isn't interested in another date."

Lacy rolled her eyes. "Then he wouldn't have said he would call you."

"When you and Neil first started seeing each other, he wouldn't leave you alone. Remember how many times a day he texted you?"

"That's true, but it was a different season of life. Neither you nor Liam are swimming in free time. You don't get off work until after ten. I don't think it's personal that he hasn't asked you on another date yet. I think you're both busy adults with full lives. Dating in our thirties is different than it was in college."

"I guess so," Hannah said.

She knew these last couple of weeks had been busy for Liam with several firefighters out sick, plus needing to take his grandfather to several routine doctors' appointments. It was possible that Lacy was right and the delay in scheduling a second date was really about Liam's personal and work life both being really busy. All of this was on top of the volunteer work he did at church. It was one of the things she liked best about him, how much time he gave to taking care of others.

And yet, it was hard to silence that tiny voice that kept saying, "You've made this mistake before—imagining a man likes you as much as you like him. Don't make it again."

The back door of Lacy's house opened, and out stepped her husband, Neil, dressed in blue jeans and a loose-fitting flannel shirt.

"Morning, Hannah," Neil greeted her.

"Good morning."

"Chillier out here than I expected." He turned from Hannah to Lacy, and his smile went from friendly to affectionate. Hannah delighted in seeing her best friend so well loved.

Lacy chucked another handful of feed into the yard. "I told you it was going to be cold today."

Neil frowned. "Did you?"

"Yes," Lacy said with a smile. "And you even said 'okay,' but you were reading. I knew you might not have actually heard me."

Hannah's cell phone buzzed in the back pocket of her jeans. Her instinct was to think *Please, Lord, let it be Liam!* She was glad only God could know that was her first thought, because it made her sound like a teenager with a crush.

But the number and name on the screen said *Amelia Jacobsen*, which was strange. Hannah couldn't remember Amelia ever calling her.

She answered at once. "Hello?"

"Hannah?" Amelia's voice had a raspy sound to it, as it had yesterday when she'd been crying. "Sorry to bother you on a Saturday morning."

"You're not bothering me. Is something wrong?"

"Am I remembering correctly that your uncle is a plumber?"

"He's retired, but yes. He's a plumber. Do you want me to call him for you?"

"Would you mind?" Her voice shook. "I'm not sure what happened, but the shutoff valve in one of the bathrooms must have malfunctioned. There's water everywhere, and the only way Isaac and I can get it to stop is when we turn off the water entirely. I tried Jason, but he isn't answering his phone, and it's impossible to do anything with the water off. I don't know what else to do."

Hannah didn't know who Jason was—perhaps the general contractor—but it didn't matter, because it didn't change what needed to be done. "I'll call Uncle Gordon and see if he can come over."

"Bless you, Hannah." Amelia's words were watery.

"Don't worry, Amelia. We'll get this taken care of."

When Hannah hung up, it was clear from Lacy's and Neil's expressions that they'd been listening to her half of the conversation and were concerned.

"Some kind of leak at Sally's B&B," Hannah explained as she pulled up Uncle Gordon's contact information. "Amelia wanted to know if Uncle Gordon could help."

"That poor woman," Neil said with a shake of his head. "It's been one thing after another for her."

Lacy nodded. "I hoped it would get better after she parted ways with Adam, but there's so much that can go wrong with a big renovation like that."

When Hannah had remodeled the old fire station to turn it into the Hot Spot downstairs and her living space upstairs, it had felt like a project that would never be done. She knew logically that the construction work would eventually end, but at the time it had felt as if she would forever be running to the hardware store or coordinating contractors or making decisions about wall colors and light fixtures. She could fully empathize with how emotional Amelia had been on the phone, because even a leaky shutoff valve—an easy fix—could feel heavy when there was yet another thing that needed to be taken care of.

She always loved the sound of Uncle Gordon's baritone voice, but it sounded exceptionally warm today when she needed him and he answered, "Hello, Hannah."

"Good morning, Uncle Gordon. I have a favor to ask."

Forty-five minutes later, Hannah pulled into the driveway of the B&B and parked behind Uncle Gordon's pickup truck. Seeing that her uncle had already arrived helped ease some of her concern for Amelia. Today she felt comfortable walking inside. While yesterday the place had smelled of sawdust and melted butter, today it smelled like damp cardboard. That wasn't good.

"Hello?" Hannah called out.

There was no response. After a moment, she could hear her uncle's voice coming from upstairs. Hannah loved the grandeur of the house's curving staircase, and she hadn't yet had the chance to walk up it. As she did so, she could hear Uncle Gordon speaking in a reassuring tone, and Hannah followed the sound of his voice down the hall and past bedrooms, resisting the urge to peek inside. There would be time for that later.

When she finally located the right room, her smile died. Several rag rugs hung on crates, with loud oscillating fans blowing on them. There were wet, dirty towels heaped in a laundry bin, evidence of a stressful Saturday morning.

She couldn't yet see Amelia or Uncle Gordon, but she could hear the distress in Amelia's words as she said, "I don't understand. Jason said he checked everything after he turned the water back on yesterday and nothing was leaking."

"Sometimes leaks are slower to form," Isaac said in a soothing voice. "Right?"

"Well, they *can* be." Uncle Gordon didn't sound convinced. "But I'm not so sure about a leak on this scale."

Hannah stepped around a heap of towels and into the bathroom. Uncle Gordon saw her and gave her the closed-mouth smile that he typically only used for somber occasions. Amelia and Isaac, who'd been standing side-by-side, turned toward her. Amelia's eyes were puffy, and Isaac's mouth was set in a grim line.

"You didn't need to drive over here," Amelia said as she folded Hannah into a hug.

"I know, but you sounded worried on the phone, and I wanted to see if I could help."

"You're the sweetest." Amelia wiped her cheeks. "I know we always say that the Lord won't give us more than we can handle, but it sure feels like I'm at capacity."

"The water damage could be extensive," Isaac said. Gone was the bravado of yesterday, when he'd assured his aunt that her fears about the bitter bride were unfounded.

"It would've been much worse if you hadn't discovered the leak when you did." Amelia added another dripping towel to the laundry bin. "But I don't understand how it could've happened. Jason told me that he fixed this sink yesterday morning."

Uncle Gordon got to his feet. "I've gone over everything, and the only thing wrong was this loose shutoff valve." He frowned at the offending plumbing. "Jason wouldn't have left it like this. He would have shut off the water to fix the sink and then turned it on again afterward. He never would have left without coming back up here and making sure everything was okay."

"So what are you saying?" Hannah asked.

Uncle Gordon shook his head. "I don't want to accuse anyone. But whoever did this did it after Jason fixed the sink. And if they didn't want to get wet, they would've had to turn the water off, come back in here to loosen the shutoff valve, and then turn the water on again. It's like it was done on purpose." He shrugged. "I don't know for sure, of course." His gaze shifted between Amelia and Isaac. "But I think it's a question worth asking."

"It's true," Isaac said, nodding his head in reluctant agreement. "The water was spraying when I came in here." Hannah looked closer and saw that his shirt was wet.

Her mind whirred with questions. "Can you tell at all when the leak started?" she asked her uncle.

He turned solemn eyes on her. "From the extent of the damage I can see, I would say that it was done sometime yesterday. There's a lot of damage in here. We need to check the rooms below this one, and then I can give you a more accurate estimate."

Isaac emitted a gruff laugh. "But why would anybody do this?"

Hannah's mind instantly went to the scorned bride from yesterday. "What was it that woman said yesterday as she was leaving?"

"Violet said this wasn't over," Amelia said thickly. "That she'd make me pay."

Hannah grimaced at the scene around her. At the soaked drywall and subfloor. At her uncle, one of several professionals who would need to be hired to get this cleaned up. Would Amelia have to push back the opening yet again? If this was what Violet meant by making Amelia pay, she'd certainly hit where it hurt.

The group went downstairs, searching for evidence of water damage as they waited for the contractor to arrive. Now that Amelia was doing something rather than simply watching Uncle Gordon, her face had taken on a firm resolve.

But her expression twisted with dismay when she realized that the leak was directly over the walk-in pantry. "Oh dear."

As Amelia opened the door, Hannah's imagination conjured up water dripping from the ceiling and bags of ingredients ruined. To her relief, Amelia flipped on the light and the room looked fine.

"It doesn't smell normal," Amelia said, wrinkling her nose.

Uncle Gordon helped himself to the stepladder leaning against a shelf and felt the ceiling. "Damp. You might need to take out this section of the ceiling and let it dry thoroughly." He glanced around at the sacks of flour and sugar. "But it could've been a lot worse. If the leak had gone on much longer, your ceiling would've collapsed, and all your food might have been ruined."

"Thank You, Lord," Amelia said.

"Indeed," Hannah murmured, and Isaac nodded.

Uncle Gordon climbed down from the ladder. "If you have another fan, I can rig it to help dry out the ceiling."

"All of mine are in use upstairs. Isaac, do you have any?"

"I do. Just give me a minute." Isaac headed for a back door. Through the glass, Hannah watched him go into a small, square house.

"That was the gardener's house when the place was originally built. It's nice that Isaac can have his own space so close." Amelia nodded down the hall. "I live in what was the cook's quarters, according to my mother."

Hannah tried to imagine what it would be like to reside in a house so big it required a live-in staff. "I wish I could have seen it when it was first built."

"Me too." Amelia looked around wistfully. "They don't build them like this anymore, with all this attention to detail."

"They also leave out the lead paint and the asbestos though," Uncle Gordon pointed out. "That's something."

Amelia grinned. "True. Fortunately, the people who bought the place from my grandparents took care of all that fun stuff."

"I'll go get the water turned back on," Uncle Gordon said as he left the room.

"For my own curiosity," Hannah said to Amelia, "would you mind telling me about your family's timeline in this house?"

"Sure. My mom grew up here and lived in this house until she married my dad. He was in the Navy, so we moved quite a bit. If I'm remembering the dates right, we were living in California when my grandparents died. I was about two, and Timmy was a newborn. Keeping the house wasn't an option at the time, but my mother always hoped to own it again someday."

"And she did," Hannah said with a smile. She loved a happy ending.

But Amelia frowned. "I wish her health had stayed better for longer. That she could've turned this place into what she'd always dreamed it would be."

"You're doing it now," Hannah said. "She'd be so proud of you."

"I'm *trying* to do it now." Amelia's gaze caught on something outside. Isaac was coming back with an old box fan in his hands. "And I want so badly to build something special with Isaac so this house can carry on to another generation of Jacobsens."

"That's a lovely goal to have."

Amelia smiled but shook her head. "Maybe. Some days this place feels like it's throwing one obstacle after another at me. I can't help but think sometimes that it might have been wiser to buy Blackberry Inn and skip all the remodeling."

"Would Sabrina have really sold her parents' place?" Hannah asked.

Sabrina Hill had taken over the historic Blackberry Inn when her parents moved to Michigan to retire close to their other daughter and her small children. Sabrina was in her early thirties and originally seemed enthusiastic about taking over the business. But a hailstorm the previous year had necessitated a new roof, which siphoned away all the money earmarked for a remodel. On top of that, Sabrina had gone through at least two managers since Hannah had been back in Blackberry Valley.

"She definitely would have." Amelia walked along the shelves of ingredients, running her fingers over them to confirm they were dry.

"She outright asked me if I wanted to buy an established place instead of opening something new. Though it needs some expensive updates, Blackberry Inn is a lovely, historical property. But my dream was never to own just any bed and breakfast or inn. The dream was specifically to open Sally's, and that can only happen here."

"Sounds like you made the right choice then."

Amelia's gaze moved to the damp ceiling. "Hopefully."

Isaac came in and scanned the room, likely searching for the best place to plug in his fan. "I can't figure out when Violet would've been able to pull a stunt like this."

"When I got back from the store yesterday afternoon, she was already here," Amelia said. "The door's unlocked, so anyone could've come in. And we didn't see her leave."

Hannah remembered the blaze in Violet's eyes and the slam of the front door. "I saw her leave."

"In that case, she probably loosened the valve before you came home," Isaac said, his back to them as he angled the fan toward the ceiling. "That might've been the real reason she was here."

Amelia frowned. "But Gordon said Jason would have noticed before he left for the day."

"Jason was gone by then, wasn't he?" Isaac asked.

"I don't think so." Amelia frowned. "It's hard to remember for sure, but he was the last one here, and I think he left around four thirty."

Hannah tucked a stray strand of hair behind her ear. "Uncle Gordon mentioned a Jason. Is he someone you've hired to fix the plumbing before?"

Amelia shook her head. "Jason is my general contractor. And I can't imagine he'd do anything like this."

Hannah thought back to yesterday's meeting with Amelia. "There were a couple of vehicles when I arrived here yesterday, but when I left at four, there was only a white Ford pickup."

Amelia nodded. "That's Jason's."

"Maybe one of Jason's employees left the shutoff valve too loose," Isaac suggested.

Amelia appeared to think about this. "I guess it's possible, but why would they, if Jason is the one who worked on the sink?"

"You know who else was here yesterday?" Isaac turned to them, a grimace on his face. "Adam Bristow."

"Adam?" Amelia's voice lifted with surprise. "Why was he here?"

Isaac shrugged. "I don't know. I only saw him as he left. Not sure how long he'd been here."

This was clearly unwelcome news. Hannah knew that Adam Bristow was the original contractor Amelia had worked with. Adam was in his late forties and had grown up in Blackberry Valley. Hannah didn't know him personally, but because of her dad being an electrician and Uncle Gordon a plumber, she knew most of the contractors in the area, at least by reputation. Adam Bristow was known for being well-priced and doing good work—if he ever got around to the job. When left to his own devices, though, he often overscheduled himself and tried to do too many jobs at once. For a while, his daughter, Megan, had managed his calendar, but she'd left for college a few months ago.

"That's odd," Amelia said. "Adam has no reason to be here. What time did you see him on the property?"

Isaac clicked his tongue a few times as he thought. "Around dinnertime. I was making Bolognese and saw him out my window as he walked toward his truck. He'd been in the backyard, based on the direction he came from, but I didn't see what he was doing. All I saw was him getting into his truck and driving away."

"Why would he have been here?" Amelia asked again, sounding as though she was talking more to herself than the two of them. "I fired him months ago."

Hannah had no answers, but Adam Bristow was a regular at the Hot Spot, and she was determined to learn more.

Chapter Three

Blackberry Valley
October 7, 1940

The schoolhouse that stood on the edge of Blackberry Valley was Sally Arterburn's least favorite place in the world, and yet she had to spend hours upon hours of her day there. This was one of the many challenges of being eleven that her parents just didn't seem to understand. Papa would frown and say, "Well, Sally, do you think I like working every day? Sometimes we have to do things we don't want to do."

But at least he'd gotten to choose his job. Sally didn't get to choose anything. She certainly hadn't been given a choice when her parents decided to leave Louisville society and build their estate in the rural hills of Kentucky.

Mama always told Sally that Miss Banks had her hands full with all those pupils and that she wasn't to cause trouble. Sally wasn't trying to cause trouble, and

Miss Banks might be capable enough to teach the youngest students, but it wasn't Sally's fault that she was better at math than the teacher. Why should she apologize for pointing out mistakes that Miss Banks made? Wasn't that being helpful? Otherwise, the other kids would learn to do math wrong. And Sally certainly wasn't going to back down when Miss Banks—wrongly—insisted that she was right.

Sally loved learning, but so far it seemed Miss Banks had nothing to teach her.

Monsieur Antoine, on the other hand, had opened up the world to her. He was the reason Sally ran all the way home as fast as she could, her lunch pail clutched in one hand and banging against her hip, her two braids bouncing on her back.

Monsieur Antoine was the Arterburn family's chef. He'd come with them from Louisville, but he was originally from France. According to the grown-ups, it was very good that he was here and not there, because of a war that was happening over in Europe. Sally only knew bits and pieces about the war and that all the adults seemed very concerned about it. What she knew was that it was good Monsieur Antoine was here, because he was teaching her how to cook and—best of all—to bake.

Last week, over the course of two days, Monsieur Antoine had taught her to make the most divine beef stew—*boeuf bourguignon*, he had called it. And there was nothing like a baguette to go with it. Sally's baguette hadn't turned out as crusty and perfect as Monsieur Antoine's, but he assured her that was part of learning.

Learning how to cook was fun, but learning how to bake made Sally feel fizzy with happiness. In addition to baguettes, she'd also learned how to make several kinds of pastries that Monsieur Antoine called *tartes*. *Tarte tatin, tarte citron,* and *tarte chocolat.* The last one was Sally's favorite. She loved chocolate so much that she sometimes daydreamed about it, the way other girls at school dreamed of falling in love or having a house of their own. When Sally was an adult, she would eat all the chocolate she wanted.

"*Bonjour,* sweet Sally," Monsieur Antoine greeted her as she burst through the back door. He spoke in a rich, deep voice and a thick accent. "How was school today?"

"Boring." Sally bumped the door closed with her hip and carried her lunch pail to the counter.

Antoine made a tsking noise. "Such a smart girl. So sad that you do not enjoy school."

Sally shrugged. Not liking school was just a fact of life, nothing to be sad about. "What are we making today?"

"Today we are making *Chausson aux pommes.* The Antoine version." He smiled at her. "When I was a young chef in Burgundy, I began to add not just cinnamon to my apples, but a blend with coriander and nutmeg as well. When Emilien saw this, he scoffed, but when he opened his bakery, what do you think made his *Chausson aux pommes* taste so good?"

"Coriander and nutmeg," Sally guessed as she tied her apron strings.

Stories of Emilien were part of the fun of working in the kitchen with Monsieur Antoine. The two had been peers at the first restaurant where they worked and shared a room at a boardinghouse, but Antoine was promoted first. Antoine said that was when Emilien became envious and wasn't as friendly anymore. Then a few months later, Antoine was promoted again.

One day soon after, Antoine came home and found that Emilien had stolen the recipes Antoine had been working on and had left town. When Emilien opened his own bakery several years later, it had been Antoine's creations that had set him apart and won him critical acclaim.

"And that is why I now keep my recipes here instead," Antoine told Sally repeatedly, tapping on his heart. "This is where good food comes from. And nobody can take this from you."

But Sally could not possibly remember everything Antoine taught her, so after each training session in the kitchen, she would hide herself away in her room and copy out everything she could remember on note cards. Someday she would have a restaurant of her own, and she wasn't going to have ordinary food like venison stew and fried chicken. She would make *coq a vin* and *cassoulet* and *boeuf bourguignon*. She would be especially famous for her desserts, and people from all over Kentucky would come to eat her cookies and tarts.

And how they would beg for the recipes. "Please, Sally," they would say to her, "won't you tell us how to make your famous *tarte chocolat*?" But Sally wouldn't tell them. She knew from Antoine how important it was to keep her creations a secret.

Someday perhaps, if she bothered with marriage and having children, she might have a son or a daughter to bring into the kitchen with her. She would teach them to cook and bake exactly the way Monsieur Antoine was teaching her now. And if she did, she would pass on her recipes in the safest way—side-by-side, working together.

The Hot Spot was the place to be on Friday and Saturday nights in Blackberry Valley, and Hannah found herself helping Jacob with prep in the kitchen. She didn't miss being a head chef, but it was nice to dip back into that world. Even if the tasks she was performing were more suited for a sous-chef, she'd always loved the rhythm of a well-functioning kitchen, and it made her feel proud that she'd created one in her hometown.

"Did you look at the videos I sent you about dry-aged steaks?" Jacob asked as he pulled pork chops off the grill.

"Not yet," Hannah said.

"I sent you three videos. I think the second one—the guy from Kansas City—is probably the direction we should go as far as methodology."

"I'll watch them," Hannah said. "But I'm worried about price. It seems like we'd have to charge so much that nobody would—"

"No, it'll be fine," Jacob assured her. "After people taste how good they are, they'll be lining up outside for the chance to pay for them."

If her waiter, Dylan Bowman, hadn't come into the kitchen to collect the Smokin' BBQ Sliders appetizer she had just finished arranging, Hannah would have pressed the issue with Jacob. The man knew what he was doing with food, and she had no doubt that his dry-aged steaks would be phenomenal, but brushing off financial decisions and focusing solely on an interesting, flavorful menu was what put many restaurants in trouble. Hannah loved unique dishes as much as the next restaurateur, but they would never stay in business if she allowed Jacob to pursue his every food interest.

When the rush had passed, Hannah left the kitchen to check on her patrons. Earlier in the week she and Elaine had decorated the Hot Spot for Christmas, and Hannah thought the place could pass for a movie set. They'd strung twinkle lights between the exposed beams and hung oversize ornaments from the ceiling, which had involved a lot of up and down on the ladder. She and Elaine had spent far too long figuring out how to wind a coiled fire hose, wrap it in Christmas lights, and hang it like a giant wreath in the front window, but the result was worth it.

Elaine stood at the hostess stand, updating the table map. Her brown hair, threaded with silver, was pulled up in a loose knot on the crown of her head, showing off her dangly silver earrings. Hannah had gotten out of the habit of wearing jewelry or nail polish—neither were great in a kitchen—but she frequently admired the extra touches of care Elaine took with her appearance. Of course, Elaine could wear a beekeeper suit to work and still manage to look lovely and fashionable.

"How are things going tonight?" Hannah asked.

"Good." Elaine finished marking the tables before looking up. "Busy, obviously. But it's Saturday, so that's to be expected. I think we're through the bulk of it."

Hannah cast her gaze around the room, enjoying how the Christmas lights made everybody's face glow in a warm, inviting way. "We did a nice job in here."

"Absolutely. I've lost track of how many compliments I've heard from people coming in. Including…" Elaine nodded toward one table.

Hannah followed the subtle point and inhaled swiftly at the sight of Liam's profile. He was there with two others from the firehouse, and they were all dressed in their uniforms.

"Are you going to go say hello?" Elaine asked pointedly.

Hannah's stomach gave a nervous flutter. "I'm going to make a loop around the room, yes."

She glanced once more at Liam, and her heart sped up when she found him already looking at her. He grinned and waved. Hannah did the same, hesitated a moment, and then crossed the room to his table. The other two firemen turned to see who Liam had waved at, and Hannah recognized Archer Lestrade—Liam's best friend—and Colt Walker.

"Hey," Hannah said, trying not to look at Liam for overly long. "How's dinner tonight?"

"Great," Liam said, gesturing to his Five Alarm Burger. "As always."

Hannah was grateful that in the low light of the Hot Spot, others might not be able to tell that she was blushing.

"Slow night at the firehouse?" she asked, making eye contact with the other two men as well.

Archer had ordered the wings—hopefully he'd been given the right ones and not the Infernos—and Colt the Rookie Meltdown, which made her smile, since he was the rookie at the firehouse. Hannah frowned at Colt's empty water glass and scanned the room for Dylan. When she spotted him chatting with a table of four women who all had full water glasses, she waved him over.

"Normal night," Liam said with a shrug. "It's *not* a slow night around here though. You guys are packed."

"Yeah, this is the first I've been out of the kitchen since about five." Hannah smiled at Dylan and gestured to Colt's empty glass.

"Oops. I'll go get the pitcher." He whirled around and narrowly escaped colliding with Raquel as she walked by with a tray of entrées. Raquel, who was used to working with Dylan, had deftly protected her tray.

Hannah watched Dylan hurry to the drinks station. "Sorry about that."

Colt shrugged. "No problem."

Anybody who frequented the Hot Spot knew what to expect from Dylan. He was eager and friendly, but patrons sometimes had to flag him down to get a refill or pay the check. He was getting better though. Hannah couldn't remember the last time he'd spilled something on a customer.

"The place looks really nice," Liam said, and Hannah felt her blush deepen. "I like what you did with that old fire hose."

"Thank you." Hannah grinned. The antique fire hose had been a loan from Liam. "I think it's fitting and festive."

"Very." Liam's dark eyes rested on her. "Are you very busy this coming week?"

Hannah's cheeks heated again. Was he asking for the reason she hoped? She glanced at Archer and Cole in time to see them exchange knowing smiles, and hope fluttered in her heart.

"No." Hannah moved to tuck hair behind her ears, despite her hair being pulled back. "I mean, no busier than usual. I'll be here all my regular times this week. The Christmas toy drive has started at church, so Wednesday morning there's a meeting about that. That'll be most Wednesdays, actually. I'll have some extra office hours because I really need to place an order. But I'm not *too* busy."

The corner of Liam's mouth lifted in a teasing smile. "Yeah, sure sounds like you'll be pretty bored. But maybe you could squeeze in a lunch one day this week?"

Hannah nodded because she was afraid her "yes!" would come out embarrassingly enthusiastic.

"Maybe Monday?"

Usually, Hannah's Mondays were pretty clear. "Well, that's when I'm supposed to help Lacy paint her guest room before Neil's family comes in for Christmas. But I could do Tuesday?"

"I work Tuesday, and we're short-staffed. Wednesday?"

"Wednesday should work. Oh, although it's Miriam's birthday. After our meeting about the Christmas toy drive, a few of us are going to take her out to celebrate. I think that would be done by twelve thirty, though, and then I could meet you somewhere?"

Liam's grin widened. "For a second lunch?"

Hannah grinned back at him. "I like food."

"What about coffee instead of you having to force down an entire meal? Jump Start at twelve thirty?"

Hannah had a meeting with her dairy supplier at two on Wednesday, but Jump Start was so close to the Hot Spot that she should be able to make that work. "Yes, that sounds great."

Hannah stepped aside as Dylan arrived with the water pitcher, his elbows jutting out farther than seemed necessary. "Sorry to keep you waiting," he said, and the water sloshed into Colt's glass in a way that made Hannah's blood pressure rise.

"Good to see you all," Hannah said, glancing at Liam one more time, relishing the warmth of his smile. "Enjoy the rest of your meal."

Hannah felt sure she was beaming as she cleared dirty plates from a table and then gestured Dylan and his water pitcher toward another half-empty glass. At last, she and Liam had another date on the calendar. As soon as she had a free moment, she'd text Lacy to tell her the good news.

Hannah stayed busy bussing tables for a while. She paused at a window table where a plate of Smokin' Sliders had been picked clean. "May I get this out of your way?"

"Sure, thanks," the man said.

When he looked up, Hannah realized that it was Adam Bristow, Amelia's original contractor. She hadn't recognized him, because usually she saw him picking up a to-go order and wearing a Kentucky Wildcats cap. Tonight he was eating with a woman who appeared the right age to be his mother.

"This is one of my favorite appetizers," Hannah said, smiling at the pair of them. "How was it?"

"Great," Adam said at the same time the woman said, "I'm a vegetarian."

"Oh," Hannah said. "Then I hope you ordered our cauliflower steak, because it's delicious."

"It was the only vegetarian entrée on the menu," the woman said with a sniff. "That and the pasta, and I don't like spicy foods."

"You'll have to come back in the summer," Hannah said. "We have more variety then, thanks to our wonderful local farmers. But I'm not a vegetarian, and the cauliflower steak is still one of my favorites."

The woman seemed not to hear—or not to care—and pushed away from the table. "Where do you keep your ladies' room?"

Hannah gestured to the hallway. "Right down that hall, ma'am."

When she'd gone, Adam cast her a tired smile. "Sorry about my mother. She's actually in a pretty good mood tonight."

Hannah didn't want to think about what Adam's mother must be like when in a bad mood. "No problem. I appreciate the feedback, actually. Jacob has been after me to add a few more vegetarian options, so he'll be pleased to hear about this. How are you these days?"

Adam shrugged. "Things are pretty good. I'm working on a house remodel in Cave City right now. You probably already know that I'm not working with Amelia anymore."

Hannah nodded. "I'm sorry that didn't work out."

"It's fine. The Cave City job is…" Adam's face reddened, and he wiped his palms on his jeans. "It's a good job. I like it. The customer is great."

"Okay." Hannah couldn't tell if he really liked the job or if he was trying to convince her that he did. "Are you completely done at the B&B, or are you still involved with some parts of it?"

Adam shook his head. "Completely off."

Then why had Isaac seen him at Sally's on Friday evening? Hannah toyed with the idea of asking, but she couldn't think of a plausible reason for doing so.

"You don't happen to know anyone who's looking for some part-time secretarial work, do you?" Adam asked. "I've had a hard time managing my calendar since Megan left for college. If I could find some good help, I think I could get back on track."

"I'll ask around," Hannah said. "I'm sure somebody in town would be happy to earn some extra cash."

"Let me know what you hear," Adam said over his glass of sweet tea. "I know you and Amelia are friends. Do you know if she's happy with Jason's work?"

The question sounded neutral, but did Hannah detect an edge in his voice? "As far as I know, yes."

Adam's jaw clenched, and he nodded. While Hannah had heard mixed reviews about Adam's time management and ability to complete a project on time, she'd never heard anything negative about his character or the work itself. Would he really have messed with the shutoff valve because Amelia fired him? This wasn't the first project he'd been fired from, and she'd never heard that he'd been vengeful about the other times.

Hannah decided to probe a bit further. "I don't know if it has to do with Jason, but some of the plumbing leaked overnight."

If Adam was surprised, he didn't show it. Although it was clear he was trying not to show emotion at all. "I'm sorry to hear that. Any damage?"

Hannah wasn't sure what to make of his flat tone. "It's too early to tell."

"These things can happen in older houses." Adam took a gulp of his tea then said, "Hope the damage is minimal."

Hannah was still considering how to reply when his mother shuffled back to the table.

"Nice bathrooms," she said. Apparently, she *was* capable of saying something positive. "Your soap smells like candy canes."

"'Tis the season," Hannah said, stepping aside as Raquel arrived with a tray. "Enjoy your meal."

Hannah carried the empty appetizer platter back to the kitchen. As she loaded dirty dishes into the dishwasher, her mind kept replaying her conversation with Adam. Of how carefully he'd guarded his emotions. Was it possible that Adam, in his anger at losing a job, had snuck in and loosened the shutoff valve?

If he had, how could she prove it?

Chapter Four

Hannah needed a rain jacket to go to church Sunday morning, but by early afternoon the sun was out and the weather was too beautiful to stay indoors. She called Lacy to see if she wanted to take a walk at a nearby trail, and fortunately Lacy agreed.

While Hannah's job kept her mostly inside, Lacy owning Bluegrass Hollow Farm meant she was outside nearly all day long. Sometimes as Hannah reached the point in her day where she was antsy to get out in the fresh air, Lacy was equally antsy to get inside and relax with a good book or a puzzle.

Hannah tightened the laces on her walking shoes and drove to Lacy's house. Fifteen minutes later, they were out in the serene hills. The trail was well marked, and though there were no leafy trees or wildflowers to enjoy this time of year, the sun was warm and the air smelled of pine.

For the first mile of their walk, Hannah told Lacy about seeing Liam the night before and the date they had planned for Wednesday.

"I'm glad you have something on the books," Lacy said. "Do you feel better now?"

"I do." Hannah tucked her hands in the pockets of her jacket. "I guess I was worried that he'd changed his mind about me. That maybe he didn't enjoy our date as much as I did."

"I assumed that's what you were worried about, but that's obviously not what happened."

"It's happened to me before," Hannah said. "With Marcus."

Lacy patted her arm. "I know."

Hannah had told Lacy about Marcus, the prep cook she'd dated not long after starting at her first restaurant in LA. She had gone on several dates with him, but each date was spread apart by weeks or more. She'd assumed the infrequency was because they were both busy and working challenging jobs. She hadn't realized that Marcus actually wasn't interested in her the way she was him. Even thinking of it now, a decade later and far away from LA, the embarrassment swamped her.

"Liam isn't Marcus," Lacy said, her tone kind but firm. "He doesn't play games."

Hannah appreciated the thought but couldn't resist pushing back a little. "You never met Marcus," she pointed out. "You have no idea what he was like."

"True," Lacy admitted. "But Liam is very honest, and I can't remember him ever being in a serious relationship before. If he wasn't interested, I think you would know."

Liam *was* honest and direct. If he decided he wasn't interested in her, Hannah couldn't imagine that he would start dodging phone calls and eating elsewhere. He would simply tell her. He would be kind, but there would be no ambiguity.

Hannah's stomach twisted as she imagined how uncomfortable that conversation would feel. She shook her head. It was silly to worry about. After all, "each day had enough troubles of its own," as

Pastor Bob had reminded them in the morning's sermon. Time to put her thoughts in a more productive place.

"You know who else was at the restaurant last night? Adam Bristow. I talked to him about what happened at Sally's."

Lacy laughed. "Of course you did."

"He brought it up, actually. He asked me if Amelia was happy working with Jason. I mentioned the water leak, and he didn't seem surprised about it." Hannah considered this for a moment. "But to be fair, he also seemed like he was trying to not show any emotion. Almost as if he was hiding something."

"Well, that could be," Lacy said, her words slow and thoughtful. "Or it could be something that's between Adam and Jason."

Hannah frowned. "What do you mean?"

Like Lacy, Hannah had grown up in Blackberry Valley and knew many people and their history, but she'd also missed quite a bit in the years she'd been gone. Sometimes Lacy had to help fill in gaps for her.

"You probably already know Adam's reputation. When he's on top of it, the job gets done well, on time, and for three-quarters of what Jason charges. But you don't know which Adam you'll get. Sometimes he gets the work done right and on schedule, and other times projects stretch on forever or things don't get ordered like they should. He's lost a number of clients to Jason over the years, from what I hear. Oh, and Jason married Adam's high school sweetheart," Lacy added. "I don't know if that contributes to their rivalry—or the one-sided rivalry, really—but I can't imagine it helps."

"I wouldn't think so." She nodded thoughtfully. "I knew about Adam having trouble with scheduling and getting projects done on time. In fact, he asked me if I knew of anyone who wanted a part-time job to help him with that. But I didn't know about the high school girlfriend thing."

Hannah turned this information over in her mind as they reached the top of the hill. The valley lay below them, picturesque in the sunshine.

"Beautiful," Lacy declared. "What a great day. I can almost forget I haven't even started my Christmas shopping."

"Tomorrow is supposed to be chilly and windy," Hannah said. "You can shop then. After we finish painting, I mean."

"I appreciate you helping me. Neil is a dreadful painter."

"Is he? I would've guessed he's a very tidy and precise painter."

"Oh, he is. He does the trim work with no tape and no mistakes. But it takes him about a week, and it makes me crazy."

Hannah snorted a laugh. That sounded right.

As they headed back down the hill, Hannah's thoughts returned to the situation at Amelia's bed and breakfast. "Do you think Adam was asking about Jason last night more because of their history than anything that's happened specifically at Sally's?"

"Seems possible."

"Though it doesn't explain why Isaac saw Adam on the B&B property the night before the leak was discovered."

"True. Has anybody asked him?"

Hannah frowned. "Not that I'm aware of. As far as I know, Isaac saw Adam but didn't say anything to him. And it's not like they're going to call the police to come take a look at a loose shutoff valve on an active construction site."

Lacy raised her eyebrows. "When you put it that way, it sounds a little too convenient, doesn't it?"

Hannah thought for a moment. "Yeah. The damage is done, but it's not exactly a crime you can have the professionals investigate."

Lacy laughed. "Just the amateurs like you and me."

After painting at the Minyards' the next day, Hannah dropped by Sally's on a whim. She'd seen Amelia at church but hadn't had a chance to speak to her.

The only vehicle in the driveway was Amelia's SUV, so Hannah opted to knock. About thirty seconds later, Amelia opened the door with a tired smile. She had an apron on, and her gray-streaked hair was pulled back in a ponytail under a floral-print bandanna. To Hannah, Amelia looked more like she was in her early fifties than her midsixties.

"Sorry to drop in on you like this."

"If I minded people dropping in, I wouldn't be opening a bed and breakfast." Amelia stepped to the side. "Come on in. I leave the door unlocked, so you should always feel free to let yourself in."

"I wanted to see how things were going and—" Hannah inhaled deeply. "What's that delightful smell?"

"Rosemary lemon shortbread. The first batch just came out of the oven. Want to help with quality control?" Amelia winked at her.

"If I must," Hannah said with a smile. "To be a good friend and all."

"I like Mom's shortbread with strong black tea, and I have a fresh pot. Any objections to that?"

"None whatsoever."

Hannah followed Amelia to the kitchen. The box fan that Isaac had brought in Saturday still whirred in the doorway of the pantry. "Did Jason come by over the weekend?"

"He did. Thanks to Isaac catching the leak when he did, the damage isn't as bad as it could've been. Jason doesn't think repair work in the bathroom and guest room will take too long, and the pantry will also need a little work. He agreed with your uncle that it would be best to take out the damp ceiling material so everything can dry thoroughly. That's what he did this morning. Fortunately, the patching can be done later, since it isn't a guest space."

"I'm so happy to hear that," Hannah told her. "When I saw all the water on Saturday, I was really worried you were going to be delayed again."

"Me too," Amelia admitted. "And I know if that happens, the Lord will sustain me, as He always does. But I'm relieved all the same. Have a seat." Amelia gestured to several barstools. "The tea should be done steeping by now."

Hannah slid onto a barstool. "Did you ask Jason about any of his employees who might have accidentally left the valve loose?"

Amelia nodded. "He said the other two guys working with him on Friday—Gustavo and Trevon—didn't even go into that room. Jason said he was the only one in there, and he didn't touch the shut-off valve or any plumbing that day. He said the repair to the sink didn't have anything to do with the plumbing. It was a cosmetic fix on the porcelain."

"You believe him?"

"I do." Amelia drummed her fingertips on the countertop. "I don't know the other two men as well as I do Jason, but Jason said they've been working with him for over a decade and he's never had a lick of trouble with either of them. And they're booked out for the next couple of months, so why would they want to slow the project down?"

Hannah had to agree that it seemed unlikely Jason or the other contractors who worked for him would do something to intentionally damage the bed and breakfast. "I've been thinking about what Isaac said on Saturday, how he saw Adam Bristow on the property."

Amelia's face again took on a weary expression. "Me too. It's concerning, isn't it?"

"A little," Hannah admitted. "It sounds like Isaac didn't speak to him at all. Is that right?"

Amelia set two cups of tea on the counter. "That's what he said. I keep wondering if I should call Adam and ask why he was here. What do you think?"

"It probably wouldn't hurt to ask. I saw him Saturday night, actually. He was eating at the Hot Spot."

Amelia slid a warm square of shortbread onto a plate, and Hannah breathed in the aroma. She loved having friends who baked.

"Did you talk to him?" Amelia asked.

"Yes." Hannah pinched off a bite of the shortbread cookie. It tasted every bit as good as it smelled, crumbly and buttery, and the lemon and rosemary bright and fresh. "Amelia, you are so gifted."

Amelia blushed and flapped her hand in embarrassment. "Just following my mother's instructions. Speaking of which—" She scooped up an open wooden box on the counter that was full of cards yellowed with age. "Let me go put this in the safe."

"The safe?" Hannah couldn't resist asking.

"I know, it's extreme," Amelia said with a chuckle. "I blame my mother. I'll be right back."

Hannah took a full bite of the cookie. She knew it was hopeless to ask how to make it—Sally's recipes were so secret that apparently Amelia kept them locked in a safe—but she was tempted to try anyway.

Amelia returned to the kitchen a minute later. "You know how Mom was about her recipes. It's so odd to me that there's a safe in what used to be the cook's bedroom, but it's very handy."

"How interesting," Hannah said. "Is it part of the original house?"

"Yes. I had assumed my mother had it installed, since she was so paranoid in her final years. But apparently it was done at the request of the original chef. Part of his contract or something."

Hannah sipped her tea then said, "I wonder what that life was like, being a private chef."

"It's interesting to think about, isn't it?" Amelia asked as she settled onto her stool. "I don't think he was at the house very long. Mom didn't really talk about him until the end, when the dementia was truly awful. Even then, he sounded like a character from a book. She talked about Monsieur Antoine more than anybody else but Dad in her final days."

"He must have been very important to her."

"I guess. But if he was, why didn't she tell me about him before then? Isaac might be right that we should've called this place 'Secret Sally's.'" Amelia dropped a sugar cube into her tea and stirred. "You said you spoke with Adam last night. Did he say anything about being here the other day?"

Hannah considered how to answer. "It was an interesting conversation, although it raised more questions than answers."

She filled Amelia in on what had been said. The longer Hannah spoke, the firmer the line of Amelia's mouth became.

"That settles it, I suppose." Amelia raised her steaming cup of tea. "I'll have to call him and ask why he was here. Adam always seemed to have a good heart, so when Isaac brought up the possibility of his involvement Saturday, it didn't sound very likely. But the way he spoke to you—well, it sounds suspicious, doesn't it?"

"It does," Hannah agreed, polishing off the rest of her cookie.

Amelia blew across the top of her tea. "Adam being involved coincides with what Jason said too."

"Which was?"

"He was certain that he checked everything before he left. That whoever did this would've had to shut off the water and then loosened the valve or they would've risked getting themselves wet." Amelia took in a wobbling breath. "That whoever did this knew the house and wanted to cause damage."

Chapter Five

Blackberry Valley
March 8, 1941

Unlike her two best friends, Sally had never cared particularly for collecting things. Judith loved seashells and music boxes. Margaret hoarded stamps, coins, and rocks. Maybe it was because Sally felt like she already had more things than a person really ought, but she couldn't see the sense in having a box of coins she never planned to spend or music boxes that gathered dust on a shelf.

But she had begun to collect recipes. She'd even bought a pretty wooden box—probably meant to hold jewelry or something else that she had no interest in—with a red velvet lining to keep her treasured cards in. Over the last few months that she'd been in the kitchen with Monsieur Antoine, she'd amassed quite a collection. She enjoyed cooking, but baking was what she loved. She'd thought she'd burst with happiness yesterday when he told her that her baguettes were as good as his now.

And though he claimed he didn't have any of his masterpieces written down, Sally wasn't sure she believed him. How could he hold so many recipes in his head all at once?

"Practice," he told her. "Practice and working alongside someone else."

Sally didn't have much experience, but she thought she agreed with him. Miss Banks at the schoolhouse often had them read from the textbook and work on their own, but Sally did better when she could get her hands on things. Like when Monsieur Antoine let her feel what the consistency and temperature of the dough should be. She couldn't learn that from a textbook.

"Sally?"

Mother was calling her name from downstairs, but it didn't sound as though Sally was in trouble.

"I'm coming!" Sally called back.

She had been studying the recipe card she'd gotten from Mrs. Berthold, who'd brought delicious lemon bars to the church picnic. Sally suspected they could be improved upon, but she didn't know how yet. Reluctantly, she pushed the card into the box and hustled down the stairs.

Her mother was regal in appearance, even when wearing a casual at-home dress. Some of her friends' moms had started wearing calf-length or even knee-length dresses, but not Sarah Arterburn. Her skirts still swept the tops of her shoes.

"What were you doing up there?" Mother asked, not suspicious. Just curious.

"Copying a recipe."

"Oh." Mother's face said that she didn't know how to feel about Sally's chosen activity. "I see."

Mother and Papa had grown up in an era when ladies didn't cook. Especially not ones at their income level. Servants did. A lady might put together a menu for a dinner party or have her cook get a recipe from a friend's cook, but she didn't involve herself beyond that.

When Sally had explained to her parents that her interest in food was natural, that every other woman in Blackberry Valley cooked for her family and that nobody but the Arterburns had their own chef, her parents had come to see her interest in food as a byproduct of their choice to raise her away from wealthy society. An oddity, but something that would pass. Like a childhood interest in playing with dolls or jumping rope.

"Speaking of recipes, I know you've been spending a lot of time in the kitchen with Monsieur Antoine," Mother said. Then she hesitated.

Sally fought the urge to fidget. Was she in trouble for that? They'd never told her not to. "Yes."

"I called you down here to let you know that Monsieur Antoine has taken another job. He'll be leaving at the end of the week."

Sally felt as though her lungs were a pair of fireplace bellows that had been squeezed. "How can that be?" she gasped. "Did you fire him?"

"Certainly not. A wonderful opportunity presented itself, so Monsieur Antoine will be leaving for New Orleans—"

"New Orleans?" Sally cried. So far away, it might as well be France.

She knew crying was a childish thing to do for a girl who was nearly twelve, but tears stung her eyes. How could he do this to her? Why would he choose to leave? Leave *her*?

"I'm so sorry, Sally," Mother said, and she clearly meant it. "When I was close to your age, I had a beloved tutor. When she got married and moved away, it was very painful."

Mother opened her arms, and after a moment's hesitation, Sally fell into them and wept.

"I was going to learn how to make shortbread next," she said between sobs. "He said I was ready."

Mother pressed her closer. "There's still time for you to learn, Sally. There are several days before Monsieur Antoine leaves, and he's a man of his word. If he said he'd teach you, I'm sure he will."

"Your mother is right, Sally." Monsieur Antoine's deep voice entered the conversation. "I will still teach you."

Sally broke away from her mother. Monsieur Antoine stood in the doorway, dressed in his usual chef's coat and trousers. The afternoons in the kitchen were the best part of her life in Blackberry Valley, and all that would change now. No more guidance when rolling out pastries or feeling the texture of a meringue, a dough, or a crust. No more stories about Emilien, and no more passing on of the recipes stored in Antoine's heart. No more learning at his side.

They had been her happiest moments, and they were over.

Sally turned away from Monsieur Antoine and raced up the curving staircase to her bedroom.

"Sally!" her mother called. Now it was the *you're in trouble* kind of yelling. "Sally Arterburn, you get back here this instant!"

Sally decided the slam of her bedroom door was a sufficient reply.

Despite the pleading of both her parents, Sally refused to return to the kitchen. She refused to see Monsieur Antoine during his final days in Blackberry Valley.

Not until after his train had departed for New Orleans did she venture into the kitchen. The room was oddly cold, and it would be for another week until the new cook started. Sally wandered down the hall, to the bedroom that had been Monsieur Antoine's these last six months and would remain empty for the foreseeable future. The new cook was someone local who wouldn't live there.

Monsieur Antoine's room was nice. Probably better than he could afford in New Orleans, Sally thought. She felt an instant bite of guilt for being so mean-spirited.

The furniture was still there—an iron bed, a dresser, a desk. Sally frowned at the sight of an open door in the wall above the desk. Not a normal door, but a square smaller than a window. As if a box had been built into the wall.

She stepped closer and realized it was a safe. The door was open, and she looked to see if there was anything inside. There was only one thing, a notecard with a recipe written out. At the top it said: *Shortbread for Sally.*

Hannah arrived at Jump Start on Wednesday and scanned the patrons in search of Liam's black hair. No luck. The line at the register was several people long. Should she join it? She didn't expect him to pay for her coffee, but getting in line and picking out a table without him did feel a little strange, as though she was starting the date without him. She hovered awkwardly by the door instead.

Getting dressed for the date had felt complicated. She wanted to be attractive, but she'd had the meeting about the church's Christmas toy drive then lunch to celebrate Miriam, both of which would normally see her attired in jeans. From the date, she would go straight to her meeting with the new dairy supplier, someone she hadn't met before, and she wanted to appear professional. She'd ultimately decided on a pair of dark jeans and a cream-colored sweater, and she kept her blond hair loose.

Hannah checked her phone and was surprised to see that it was a few minutes after twelve thirty. In all her experiences with Liam, he'd been prompt. Maybe he'd forgotten. As she peered around the coffee shop again to make sure she hadn't overlooked him, her phone buzzed in her hand. The call was from Liam "Champion Chauffeur" Berthold, as he'd most recently saved his name in her phone.

Hannah answered. "Hey. I was wondering if you'd forgotten."

"I'm so sorry," he said in a low voice, and Hannah's hopes that the date was still going to happen vanished. "I took Gramps to his doctor's appointment and thought I'd be back in plenty of time, but they want a chest X-ray—"

"What?" Hannah couldn't help interrupting. She adored Patrick Berthold. "What's wrong?"

"Nothing to be too alarmed over. He's had a lot of congestion, and they want to make sure it hasn't turned into pneumonia. It's a precaution, but everything is taking forever. I'm hoping we can leave here in the next twenty or thirty minutes. Any chance that works for you?"

If it was that long before they left the doctor's office, Liam wouldn't be back to Blackberry Valley for another hour or so.

"I have a meeting at two, so I can't." Hannah tried not to sound as deeply disappointed as she felt.

From the counter, Zane called out, "Eggnog latte for Rose," in his booming voice.

"You're already there, aren't you?" Liam said. "Of course you are. I feel terrible about this, Hannah. I'll make it up to you."

Hannah joined the back of the line. She wasn't going to miss out on a date *and* coffee. "I understand. Your grandfather needs you."

"I assume you work tonight?"

She attempted a lighthearted laugh. "You assume correctly. Do you think Blackberry Valley would be understanding if I shut down the restaurant for a few hours so we can have a date?"

"What about— Oh, sorry. They just came to get us for the X-rays. I'll call you back in a bit."

"Okay, bye," Hannah said, but it was to dead air. She stared at the blinking "call ended" and decided to get whipped cream on her coffee.

While she waited for her order, Hannah scrolled through the pictures Drew, her brother, had sent of her niece and nephews from an ice-skating excursion over the weekend. Typically pictures of the kids were a boost to her spirit, but today they made her feel sadder. Lonelier. Would she ever have this?

It's one postponed date, Hannah Prentiss, she scolded herself. *Don't make too much of this.* And wasn't the reason she liked Liam so much *because* he was the type of man who would make sure his grandfather got to the doctor? She loved his heart for taking care of others. She just wished it wasn't getting in the way of their date.

Zane was too busy for anything more than a warm smile as he handed over her peppermint latte with extra whipped cream. Hannah thanked him and headed toward the exit, ticking through her options for how to spend her unexpectedly free hour.

She was about to exit Jump Start when she noticed Violet, the bitter bride who'd yelled at Amelia. She had a laptop open on a round table for two and tapped away at a furious pace with her long red nails. She wasn't scowling at the screen, exactly, but her brow was furrowed with intense concentration.

Hannah's heart pounded as she considered striding over to Violet's table and demanding to know if she'd tampered with the plumbing at Sally's. Would Violet even remember who Hannah was? Hannah didn't think she'd made the impression on Violet that Violet had made on her. Could she use that to her advantage? Pretend not to know Violet? But if she did that, how would she casually bring up Sally's?

Violet looked up from her screen and caught Hannah staring. She blinked a few times. "Hi. I know you."

So much for an undercover operation.

Hannah nodded and offered a slight smile, not even sure she wanted to give Violet that much. "Yes, we met a couple of days ago."

Violet winced. "Well, I'm not sure that's how I would phrase it. You saw me throwing a tantrum."

Hannah's smile broadened. There was something almost endearing about Violet admitting it. "You seemed quite upset, yes."

Violet's head tilted, as though she was studying Hannah. "Do you work at Sally's? For Amelia?"

"No. I work at the Hot Spot. Actually, I own it." Hannah drew closer to Violet's table and gestured with her peppermint latte in the general direction of her restaurant. "But Amelia is a good friend of mine."

Violet frowned. "Is that the restaurant that went in where the old fire station used to be?"

"That's right."

"I haven't eaten there yet, but I've heard good things. I don't live in Blackberry Valley."

"Where do you live?"

"Cave City."

"Did you grow up there?"

Violet's face darkened, and she averted her eyes to her computer screen. "No. That's where my college boyfriend was from, and he wanted to move back. We were engaged, so I followed him, but we..." Violet shrugged. "Things didn't work out like I thought they would. We're not engaged anymore."

Violet tapped a few keys on her keyboard, but Hannah was pretty sure that was more to escape the discomfort between them than out of actual need. When Violet wasn't scowling and stomping around, she really was beautiful. She had a lovely complexion and dark, almond-shaped eyes. Hannah wondered if she used a specific product on her hair that made it so shiny—something that Hannah could buy for her own hair—or if the shininess was just a gift from God to Violet.

"I'm sorry about your broken engagement," Hannah said. "That's really hard, especially when you moved here for him."

Violet's jaw hardened. "Everyone keeps saying it's probably for the best, but I don't see that. To me, it seems like if Sally's Bed and Breakfast had honored their word, I would be in Hawaii on my honeymoon right now instead of applying for jobs that are anywhere but around here." Violet rolled her eyes. "How is my still being in this dinky town evidence of things working out for the best?"

Hannah felt her temper flare at Violet's description of her beloved hometown but reminded herself to stay calm. "Sometimes we have to wait a while to see the good in a situation."

"I guess so." Violet raised her Jump Start cup to her mouth. "I'm sorry, I don't mean to dump my troubles on you." She made a noise that sounded like a mix between a laugh and a sob. "You must think I'm crazy."

"I think I'm meeting you when you're going through a hard season."

"That's generous. Thank you." Violet sighed. "You don't have to stay and talk to me. I know you were headed out the door."

Hannah glanced at her phone. "Actually, I suddenly have a few minutes free. At Sally's, you told Amelia and Isaac that you'd make them pay for what they did to you. I can't imagine that's the kind of thing you'd usually say."

Violet's arms crossed over her chest, and her jaw hardened once again. "I'm certainly not going to keep quiet about what happened. Consumers deserve to know the truth about them. You can book a date at Sally's, you can put down a deposit, but it doesn't guarantee you'll actually have your wedding there."

Hannah forced herself to slowly inhale through her nose. "What you need to understand is, there were circumstances out of their control—"

"That may be, but they were definitely in control of when they started accepting reservations. If Amelia thought there was a chance they wouldn't be open yet, she shouldn't have been booking events."

Hannah knew there was probably nothing she could say to smooth over the situation with Violet, because she imagined that Amelia and Isaac had tried everything already. Even still, she persisted. "I know that's frustrating, but Amelia tried to get you rebooked. She even tried to find another venue here in town for you. She feels terrible about what happened and didn't deserve to be yelled at."

Violet snorted. "She deserved that and more."

Hannah arched her eyebrows. "Like some water damage?"

Violet stared at her, open-mouthed. Her eyes still held fury, but she also looked confused. Or maybe she was faking the confusion. Hannah didn't know her well enough to be able to tell. "Water damage?"

Hannah didn't elaborate.

"I don't know what you're talking about," Violet said after a few tense moments. She adjusted her laptop and scooted her chair closer to the table. Her body language was clear. She was ready for this conversation to be over.

Hannah rested her hand on the table and waited for Violet to look up. "It seems pretty suspicious, that's all. You tell Amelia and Isaac you're going to make them pay, and the next day something goes wrong that leads to expensive repairs and yet another delay in their opening."

"That wasn't me," Violet said, her eyes wide. "I don't know a thing about that. When I said I'd make them pay, I meant with something *normal*, like an honest online review or posting on all my social media platforms about what they did to me. I'm so mad

I'd post those secret recipes she's so proud of, if I knew where to find them. But there's no way I would ever cause actual damage to the property."

Hannah crossed her arms over her chest. "I don't know. You seemed pretty mad when you left."

"Yeah, I was, but you saw me leave. And I was with somebody the entire time I was there."

"Were you?"

Violet squirmed in her seat. "Mostly, yes. When I first arrived, I waited a little while for Amelia by myself, but I was in the foyer the entire time. I wasn't wandering around looking for ways to break pipes or whatever happened."

Hannah considered Violet. She seemed to be telling the truth. And while the timing could technically work, Violet would have to have known exactly where to go to shut off the water. Then she'd have to turn it back on after loosening the shutoff valve. All without being noticed. That didn't seem very likely.

Hannah inhaled deeply. She didn't want to leave the conversation in an unpleasant place, especially since she'd told Violet that she was the owner of a restaurant. She didn't want Violet to get it into her head that she should write an "honest" online review about the Hot Spot.

"Thank you for explaining the situation to me," Hannah said in the tone she used with ruffled customers. The kind who complained because they wanted a free dessert or a comped meal. "The timing was strange, and I feel protective of my friend."

"Sure," Violet said dismissively. "I need to get back to what I'm doing now."

Well, so much for smoothing over the situation. "What kind of job are you looking for?"

"I work in retail now, but I would take anything that pays enough to get me away from the mess of my life here."

Hannah recalled that Adam Bristow was searching for a part-time employee, but as a local contractor, he wouldn't be able to offer Violet a relocation. So all she said was, "Good luck with your search."

She left the discontented young woman and headed out into the crisp, gray afternoon. "Have Yourself A Merry Little Christmas" had been playing in Jump Start, and Hannah found herself humming the tune as she fumbled to zip her coat without spilling her latte. The town decorations along Main Street, which had looked almost out of place in Sunday's fine weather, seemed much more appropriate when flapping in the brisk wind.

Hannah decided she had enough time to go to Blackberry Market and restock her personal pantry. Her shelves were looking pretty bare. As she wandered the aisles of the small grocery store, her mind kept drifting back to her conversation with Violet. To how easy it was for the young woman to convince herself that Amelia and Isaac had wronged her and that she was in the right. It didn't seem like a stretch to think that Violet could also convince herself that something like causing a leak was a justifiable action.

Hannah shook her head. Even if Violet felt she was in the right, it didn't change the fact that there wasn't enough time for her to pull off a stunt like that, not when she wouldn't be familiar with the inner workings of Sally's.

But Adam Bristow would be.

Chapter Six

When Hannah left Blackberry Market, heavy grocery bags hanging from both arms, the first thing she noticed was a dog barking incessantly nearby. She came around the corner and was immediately greeted by the source—a black-and-white short-haired dog cowering between the legs of Sabrina Hill and barking at Amelia. Sabrina was shouting, and at first Hannah thought the two women were arguing but then realized the volume was simply so she could be heard.

"It's too expensive for a bigger place like Blackberry Inn. Every choice I make about a bedroom, I have to multiply the cost by fifteen. That's significant compared to eight." Sabrina tugged at the leash. "Togo, be quiet."

Togo ignored her and kept right on barking.

"I'm so sorry," Sabrina said. "I adopted him two weeks ago. I promise he's harmless, just protective."

"I had a rescue dog once," Amelia replied at the same volume. "Sweet as could be, but they come with their own quirks, don't they?"

Sabrina took several steps. "I need to finish my walk and get back to the inn. Good talking to you."

Togo barked twice at Hannah as they passed by, but otherwise walking seemed to be the way to silence him. Sabrina waved at her with an apologetic smile but kept moving.

Amelia took notice of Hannah and gestured to her full arms. "Can I help you carry those?"

"I'm fine, thank you. It's not that far to my place. What are you up to this afternoon?"

Amelia reached for a bag, despite what Hannah had said. "Heading to the Hot Spot to find you, so let me take one of those."

"Why were you looking for me?"

"I'll tell you when we're inside." Amelia glanced around. "How was the toy drive meeting this morning? I'm hoping to be there next week."

As they walked, Hannah updated Amelia on how the discussion had gone and the plans Connie had laid out for collecting, wrapping, and distributing the toys to underprivileged children all over the county.

"Connie said she'll send out a message to those who weren't there today," Hannah told Amelia as they walked up the steps to her apartment. "Bryn was out with a stomach bug, and Vera was at home because one of her kids has the same thing. There's clearly something going around."

"It's that time of year, I suppose," Amelia said as she followed Hannah inside.

Hannah was glad that she kept her place tidy enough not to panic over an unexpected guest. Though she suspected Amelia wasn't the sort to care about a pile of clean laundry on the couch or dirty dishes in the sink. The apartment looked especially nice with the Christmas tree in the corner and garland draped around the windows.

Amelia placed the bags on Hannah's counter. "What a charming place."

"Thank you." Hannah unloaded her bag of produce into the fruit bowl. "I'm really pleased with how it turned out. You said you were coming to the Hot Spot to talk to me. Is something wrong?"

Amelia tweaked the grocery bags closest to her, lining them up so they were even with one another. "I was at Legend & Key to pick up a map Neil had ordered for Sally's, and I met Sabrina when I was loading it into my car. That's when it occurred to me—if anybody in town is motivated to keep Sally's from opening, it's Sabrina."

Hannah considered this. She and Sabrina were not close enough that Hannah would call her a friend, but they were definitely friendly. Whenever she had interacted with Sabrina at Blackberry Inn or the Hot Spot, Sabrina had always struck Hannah as someone with a good heart. Not surprising, considering Mr. and Mrs. Hill were lovely people. Yes, Hannah had heard the Hills express some concerns about Sabrina taking over the inn, but she'd also heard that was because they knew how overwhelming a job it was for one person, not because they didn't trust their daughter.

Amelia was waiting for her response.

"And you think that because she's your competition?"

"Partly. But also, remember how I told you that she asked me to consider buying the inn instead of opening Sally's?"

Hannah nodded. Her phone buzzed in her pocket, and though she was pretty sure it was Liam and she would like to answer the call, she wasn't about to interrupt Amelia. Liam would have to wait.

"She wasn't just asking. She was practically begging me to buy the place. Told me it had a new roof and that she'd already paid an interior designer to put together plans for a big remodel."

"Really?" Hannah hadn't realized Sabrina had such major renovations planned that they would require hiring a designer. She'd assumed Sabrina's intentions were more about refreshing what was already there. "What kind of remodel?"

"A few weeks ago she showed me what she was thinking, and..." Amelia grimaced.

"Not good?"

"I wouldn't say that. Just not right. She wants to change everything to an Art Deco vibe."

"Oh." Hannah frowned as she thought about the interior of Blackberry Inn. "They opened in the '40s, though, right? Isn't Art Deco more of a 1920s thing?"

"That's what I mean. The architecture is all very 1940s, so making the interior look like a hotel from the Roaring Twenties seems like an odd choice to me. I tried to gently suggest that her money would be better spent preserving the details of the decade rather than creating an Art Deco facade, but she just dismissed my concerns. Anyway, when I insisted that opening a B&B in this particular house was my mother's dream—and now *my* dream—she told me, 'I think you'll regret this decision. You don't understand all the things that can go wrong with a place like that.'" Amelia gave Hannah a pointed look.

Hannah wasn't so sure. "I'll grant that her comment didn't age well, but did you get the impression that she was threatening you? Or was she just disappointed and wanted to persuade you to change your mind?"

Amelia seemed to consider that. "At the time she said it, I thought she was just upset I didn't want to buy the inn, but now I'm wondering if it was a warning of some kind. Like, 'if you don't buy the place, I'll make sure life is really hard for you.' I tried talking to her about the plumbing mishap, hoping I could gauge her reaction, but it was impossible with her dog barking."

Hannah smiled. "Having to yell at each other isn't conducive to sleuthing."

"I'll mention my suspicions to Isaac and see what he thinks," Amelia said. "He'll probably say something about Sabrina being too busy at the inn and not having time for pranks like that. He'll say Adam has a lot more time on his hands. Isaac thinks we should look at Adam more seriously. Or Violet."

Hannah hoped Isaac had enough sense not to refer to tampering with the shutoff valve as a "prank," because that seemed like too lighthearted a word. He'd seemed to take it more seriously the day it happened.

"I just had a conversation with Violet, actually." While Hannah put away her groceries, she told Amelia about the run-in at Jump Start. "She claims she wasn't alone long enough to do any damage to the place, and that even if she had been, that wasn't what she meant about you having to pay for what you did. She said she meant to write an online review or something."

Amelia pressed her teeth into her lower lip, clearly concerned over the idea. "That could be devastating to a new place." She wrung her hands. "What a mess."

"Even if Violet did sabotage the shutoff valve, I don't know how we'd prove it," Hannah said. "Or prove that anyone did it, for that matter. Though I still think it's worth talking to Adam and finding out why Isaac saw him that night."

"I did call him. Adam said he was missing a drill and thought it might be at our place. He claims he never came inside, but..." Amelia shrugged. "Like you said, it's tough to prove. I think I believe him though."

"Why would he search for the drill outside and not bother with inside?" Hannah asked. "Wouldn't it be more likely that he'd have left a tool inside?"

"Adam claims that he texted Jason asking if the drill was anywhere inside and Jason said he hadn't seen it. Adam said he planned to call me later and ask to come when Jason wasn't there, but then he didn't need to because he found the drill later that night."

Hannah arched her eyebrows. "That's pretty convenient."

"But, as you said, how would we prove it? Even if we were convinced that it was Adam or Sabrina or Violet?" Amelia waved a hand, as if doing so could make the whole distasteful business go away. "The good news is that Jason says this won't slow us down nearly as much as he initially thought. He thinks we'll be able to open on December twenty-second as planned."

"Really?" Hannah brightened. "That's wonderful news."

Amelia grinned in return. "It is, isn't it? Isaac is such a perfectionist that he wanted to pull off a bunch of drywall to make sure all the water damage was caught. And it isn't as though I *want* mold growing in my bed and breakfast, but that would certainly cause a delay. Jason assured me it's unnecessary and we can just press on."

"What a relief." Hannah threw her arms around Amelia in a celebratory hug.

While Amelia didn't seem strapped for cash, Hannah knew her friend had invested a lot, and she couldn't start recouping her investment until the doors opened and paying guests arrived.

"I know." Amelia squeezed back. "I think the worst is behind us now."

Chapter Seven

When Lacy came into the Hot Spot to pick up her to-go order, there was enough of a lull that Hannah could fill her in on her conversation with Amelia.

"She thinks Sabrina Hill could've been involved?" Lacy frowned as she considered this and absently tugged at her ponytail. "I've chatted with Sabrina a few times during egg deliveries. I'm taking her a delivery tomorrow, actually. I don't see her doing something like that. She's…" Lacy searched for the right word. "Very put-together. Professional skirts. Nice shoes. Manicures. It's hard for me to imagine her sneaking around Sally's in her high heels or wandering down into a dank old basement to shut off the water."

Hannah held up her hands. "I'm just repeating what Amelia said. I don't know Sabrina well enough to offer an opinion on that. And I think Amelia has decided it doesn't really matter, because the bed and breakfast is going to open as scheduled after all."

"Well, that's good news. Amelia has worked so hard and persevered through so much." Lacy's frown deepened. "But I still think it matters who did this."

Hannah smiled. "This is why you're my best friend. That is the exact thought I had."

Lacy leaned against the counter, as though settling in for a long chat. "Obviously, whoever caused the leak was trying to achieve something. And presuming that 'something' wasn't for Amelia to carry on and open as planned, and since what they tried didn't work, they might try something else."

Hannah nodded. "Amelia is so focused on getting the B&B open, she doesn't want to direct any energy to finding out who did it. I think she's making a mistake, but what can I do?"

Lacy grinned. "Sounds to me like the only option is for you to keep looking into it on your own and try to figure out whodunnit before anything else happens at Sally's."

"It's as if you can read my mind," Hannah said with a laugh.

Lacy looked at her watch. "I'd better go. Neil and I have a date tonight. I want to work on my new puzzle, and he wants to read, so we're compromising. I'm going to do the puzzle while he reads aloud to me."

Hannah wasn't sure she'd ever heard of an evening that described the Minyards better. "The two of you are adorable."

"Neil even matched his reading to my puzzle. How cute is that? I'm working on a London street scene, so he selected a Sherlock Holmes story to read. I think he's even going to attempt a British accent."

Hannah pictured Neil in a deerstalker hat and chuckled. "Please try to record some of it for me."

"I'll see what I can do." Lacy waggled her fingers. "Good night, Sherlock."

"Good night, Watson."

Still smiling, Hannah ducked back into the kitchen. Wednesdays were typically slower at the Hot Spot, so she hoped to have a chance to return Liam's phone call from earlier that afternoon. But so far, she'd barely been able to string together more than a minute of solitude.

"What do you think about expanding our hours to include lunch?" Jacob asked as Hannah surveyed what he was doing and how she could best help.

She almost laughed out loud at his suggestion but then took note of his earnest expression. "What makes you ask?"

"I've been thinking a lot about sandwiches." Jacob rearranged the chicken on the grill, and Hannah took over babysitting the gravy. "There's so much variety, sandwiches could be the entire lunch menu."

"I do like sandwiches," Hannah said.

"Everybody likes sandwiches. That's what makes it a good idea. We could offer five or seven choices. Maybe ten. And then maybe a couple of soups because that's such a classic combination. You know somebody is going to order the Gouda Grilled Cheese and need a bowl of creamy basil tomato soup to go with it."

Hannah internally groaned. These conversations were even harder when Jacob was already naming menu items. Though she had to admit that a Gouda Grilled Cheese sounded delicious. She hadn't eaten since lunch with the ladies.

"And if we're going to do sandwiches and soups, it would probably be smart to offer a few salads," Jacob continued. "There are always those people who are going to want a salad."

"They aren't bad ideas, Jacob."

He gave her a sidelong glance. "But?"

Hannah sighed. "I love sandwiches and soups and salads. And I love creating new menu items, but every choice like that comes with a cost. The Hot Spot has to be profitable, or I can't pay any of you."

Jacob grimaced. "I thought you might say that."

"Write all your ideas down though," Hannah said. There was a crashing sound from the dining room that sounded distinctly like a dropped tray. "A Gouda Grilled Cheese sounds really, really good."

"On sourdough bread that we bake in-house!" Jacob called after her as she left the kitchen to help in the dining room.

Hannah wasn't surprised to find Dylan crouched over a tray. The back of his neck was bright red, but fortunately, it looked as though the dropped tray had only held drinks—not entrées that needed to be remade quickly—and nobody appeared to be wearing a splash of ice water. One of the customers was actually on her hands and knees beside Dylan, helping to corral the mess. It could have been much worse. Hannah grabbed several towels and the broom and rushed over.

"Sorry, Hannah," Dylan muttered as she approached. The poor guy seemed mortified. Hannah wanted to hug him but knew that would only make his embarrassment that much worse.

"These things happen," she said instead with a practiced, patient smile. "I've dropped plenty of trays in my time too."

"It was my fault," said the customer who was helping pick up the broken glass. "I should've looked before I scooted my chair back."

"We added an extra table for the holidays, and it's made things a bit tight in here," Hannah said. "I'll get the rest of this with the broom. I don't want anybody's hands getting cut."

Hannah shooed Dylan away to try again with the drinks and finished cleaning up the mess herself. The normal din of the dining room returned, and the sound was comforting to her soul. With the Christmas decorations hung, the soft rain falling outside, and the savory aromas of the Hot Spot, the moment felt calm and peaceful, despite the reality that she was sweeping up some of her profits.

The evening passed in a blur of tables filled and cleared and filled again. The orders came in at a steady stream that kept Jacob too busy to talk any more about sandwiches or house-made sourdough bread. When the kitchen was cleaned up, the dining room reset for the next day, and the doors locked, Hannah headed upstairs to her apartment to wind down before crawling into bed.

She considered texting Liam to explain why he hadn't heard from her, but it was after eleven, and she'd feel terrible if her text woke him. She bit her lip as she considered today's canceled date and her inability to do something simple like call him back. Was that a bad sign? Was she trying to force a relationship at the wrong time?

This was probably her long day and her fatigue talking. Just that morning, while at the Christmas toy drive meeting, the conversation had turned to the sermon on Sunday and what the Bible said about struggles. How struggle led to perseverance, perseverance to character, and character to hope. So, she wasn't trying to *force* things with Liam. She was struggling and having to persevere, the way Amelia was persevering through all the ups and downs of opening Sally's.

Hannah would persevere as well. But first she would get some sleep.

"Is it ever a challenge for you and Marshall to make time to see each other?" Hannah asked Raquel as they worked together on silverware rolls. The work was simple, and Hannah had always liked how it created space for conversations with coworkers.

Raquel tipped her head to one side, her brown, curly hair spilling over her shoulder. "Not really. I see him a lot here, of course. And since he often does his writing at Jump Start when he doesn't have to be at the office, I pop over there." She laughed. "I get up a lot earlier and drink much more coffee than I used to."

Hannah grinned at the idea of early-morning—and jittery, apparently—meetings between Raquel and Marshall. Raquel deserved a good relationship, and Hannah was delighted that the two of them were so happy together. And that she had a front row seat, since they'd met right here at the Hot Spot.

"I take it you and Liam are having a hard time connecting?" Raquel asked, her lovely dark eyes trained on Hannah.

"Well, kind of. I see him pretty often, really, but typically only here or at church. Actually finding time to go on a date—or even call each other—has been really challenging." Hannah secured the end of a napkin and added the completed roll to the pile. "And his schedule is a little hectic. It's not like the fire station is ever closed."

"I never thought about that," Raquel said. "He basically has to be available twenty-four hours a day, doesn't he?"

Hannah shrugged. "A call could always come in. Fires don't only happen during business hours."

"Wow. The downside of dating a hero, I guess."

Hannah chuckled. "I guess so."

"Well," Raquel said slowly, "I'm not sure how helpful I can be. As far as I know, there are no food-critic emergencies. Marshall's hours are flexible, and when he's trying a new place for lunch, I can go along with him."

Hannah smiled. "I can't really accompany Liam to work."

Raquel grinned. "Which is a shame. You'd look very cute in a fireman's hat."

Hannah laughed. She had called Liam back that morning and was pleasantly surprised when he answered the phone. They'd talked for an entire twenty minutes before he'd had to go to some public-safety city meeting. By the time he'd filled her in on his grandfather's appointment—not pneumonia, thankfully—and Hannah had updated him about Amelia's situation at Sally's, they only had five minutes to try and schedule a date.

Those five minutes had ended with Liam sighing and saying, "I have to go, but I'll see what kind of space I can free up next week."

Next week? That seemed so long from now. Then Hannah laughed at herself. Today was Thursday, so "next week" was really only a few days away. But still, it felt like they'd been saying "next week" for weeks now. Why was this so hard?

Hannah's phone buzzed in her pocket. She hoped it was Liam with the news that he'd found some sort of free time open tomorrow morning or this weekend.

But it was Lacy. Which was always a good thing.

"I'm on my way to make a delivery to Blackberry Inn," she said. "Any interest in joining me?"

For a moment, Hannah couldn't figure out why Lacy was asking her this, and then she put it together—it was so Hannah could talk with Sabrina.

Hannah checked the clock. "Think I'd be back here by three?"

"Absolutely," Lacy said, punctuated by a brief honking sound that Hannah heard both through the phone and through her other ear. "I just pulled up outside."

Hannah had always admired Blackberry Inn. The small hotel had been built downtown by Sabrina's ancestors, and it was bursting with charm and character. She loved the brick front, the green-striped awnings, and the old-fashioned curvy letters of the sign that read BLACKBERRY INN, ESTABLISHED 1941.

When Hannah was in high school, her mom sometimes met friends at the inn's restaurant for breakfast because back then Blackberry Valley didn't offer many options. These days the restaurant patrons were mostly guests at the inn. From the market research Hannah had done before opening the Hot Spot, the inn's menu options were small and the prices big. Hotel guests received a discount, but still, she wondered how many guests at the inn would instead go to Sally's for breakfast once they opened. And how threatening that idea must feel to Sabrina.

"Are you the good cop this time, or am I?" Lacy teased as she parked her truck alongside the delivery entrance in the back alley.

Hannah grinned. "You're the egg supplier, so if one of us is going to be the good cop, it should probably be you."

"I feel like somewhere in this conversation there's a chance to make a pun about a bad egg, but I can't think of it fast enough." Lacy set the parking brake and shut off the ignition.

Hannah laughed as she climbed down from the truck cab. "I tend to think of the really good jokes about five hours later."

"Really? I prefer two in the morning when I'm lying awake for no good reason." Lacy nodded to a crate. "Can you grab that one?"

Hannah trailed behind as Lacy headed to the entrance and then pushed the intercom buzzer with her elbow.

Lacy rested the crate on her hip. "Hopefully Sabrina's here and I didn't bring you along for nothing. Not that spending time with me isn't its own reward."

"The best reward," Hannah agreed.

The door swung open, and a woman with a heart-shaped face smiled at the two of them. "Hi, Lacy. Come on in."

"This is my friend, Hannah. She's helping me out this morning," Lacy said. "Hannah, this is Chrissy. She's the inn's general manager."

"Nice to meet you," Hannah said as Chrissy led them along the hall toward the walk-in refrigerator.

"You work at the Hot Spot?" Chrissy asked.

"Actually, I own it." Hannah wasn't surprised that Chrissy had asked. After all, she was wearing a long-sleeved shirt that said *The Hot Spot* across the front.

"I like that place a lot. I wish you served lunch."

Hannah grinned, thinking of her conversation with Jacob. "As a general manager, I'm sure you understand the trade-offs of being open additional hours."

Chrissy ushered them into the refrigerator and opened her mouth to reply, but a sharp female voice called out, "Chrissy?"

The tone reminded Hannah of hearing her mom call for her from elsewhere in the house—and knowing it wasn't going to be a pleasant conversation. Not that Hannah had gotten in trouble much as a kid, but that made the few times she had blaze all the brighter in her memory.

Chrissy offered Hannah and Lacy a tight smile. "One moment." She turned and backtracked several steps before calling back, "Sabrina, I'm in the refrigerator with Lacy and Hannah."

Hannah recognized this as code for *Be nice, we have guests.*

Footsteps echoed down the hall, and then Sabrina stepped into the refrigerator with a smile on her face. "How funny. I'm running into you everywhere these days, Hannah. Sorry I didn't stop to say hi outside the market yesterday. I'm sure you noticed that I have a new dog."

"Yes, he seemed rather opinionated." Hannah smiled and gestured to Lacy, who was finishing up her task of stacking the cartons of eggs on the shelf. "I was hanging out with Lacy and wanted to come inside the inn. I've always admired it."

Not that the view between the delivery door and the commercial refrigerator was picturesque. Hopefully Sabrina was too flattered to consider this.

"Thank you. Do you want it? I'll hand you the keys right now." Sabrina punctuated this with a laugh, but Hannah wondered how real the offer was when she thought of the things Amelia told her.

Hannah laughed too. "I struggle with all the to-do lists involved in running a restaurant, so I can't imagine taking over something like this."

"Do you really? And you're only open for dinner," Sabrina said. "You can't even imagine how much harder this is."

Hannah hesitated. While that might be true, it wasn't particularly kind.

"Any chance you have time to show Hannah around, or are you too busy right now?" Lacy asked. "I know she'd love a tour."

"Of course," Sabrina agreed at once, beaming.

"That's so kind of you," Hannah said. "I know you're really busy."

Sabrina waved for her and Lacy to follow her out of the refrigerator. "This is my favorite part of the job. I enjoy showing off the place, even if it is in desperate need of an update. I'd love to remodel and give it a cool Art Deco vibe. Something where people walk in and think, 'Wow, am I still in Blackberry Valley, or did I just walk into a Jazz Age hotel in New York City?'"

Hannah had never thought of Blackberry Inn as outdated, just historic. "That would be very different than when your parents ran the place."

"Yeah, they didn't like the idea at all when I brought it up, but the 1940s thing doesn't do it for me, you know?" Sabrina pushed the door open to usher them into the lobby. "Have you ever stayed at the Goldenrod in Louisville? It's an Art Deco-style hotel. The 1920s had so much more flare, I think. It's much more me."

That might be true, but Hannah had to agree with Amelia that it didn't fit the history of Blackberry Inn. The lobby was a mix of rich wood paneling and textured wallpaper with soft furniture scattered about. The whole room smelled of pine, thanks to the Christmas tree next to the front desk, behind which a young man stood. He was probably in his early twenties and gave them a friendly smile. While Hannah could see that some of the furniture needed some TLC and the lighting was on the dim side, the room felt warm and homey to her, especially with the fire crackling and soft Christmas music playing.

"I would rip out this whole front section." Sabrina waved to the ornate door and two front windows. "Make it all glass, so we get lots of natural light in here. And this dark wallpaper and paneling would all have to go. I found a great geometric-print paper that I'd use instead. And naturally I'd replace that awful brass chandelier."

While the chandelier wasn't something Hannah would want hanging in her apartment, she thought it was perfect for the Blackberry Inn lobby.

"That looks original," Lacy observed.

"It is," Sabrina said with a sigh. "I've always hated it, but my parents wouldn't dream of touching it, since my grandmother picked it out herself. Not that I can afford to do any of this, anyway. Replacing the roof depleted most of our savings, and the HVAC system took the rest."

Before Hannah could figure out how to reply, Sabrina scowled at a stack of mail sitting on the front desk. "Did I leave that there?"

"Yes, ma'am." The employee's gaze flicked to Hannah and Lacy before he continued. "You left it there last time you walked through. I was going to move it, but I know you don't like it when we move things."

"You could have at least moved it so it wasn't in view of guests." Sabrina gathered the pile of mail in clear irritation. "There's always so much to do. I took Friday and Saturday off last week, and I haven't fully caught up yet."

She had been off work on the day Sally's was sabotaged? The back of Hannah's neck tingled, and she glanced at Lacy, who appeared to be thinking along the same lines.

"That sounds nice," Lacy said in a bright voice. "Did you do anything fun while you were off?"

"Yes, actually. Thursday night I flew to Michigan. My sister had a baby recently, and I got to spend two entire days with him before flying home Sunday morning." Sabrina fished her phone from her pocket. "He's the cutest thing. Do you want to see pictures?"

"Sure," Hannah said, trying to keep the disappointment out of her voice. Not because cute baby pictures were ever a disappointment, but because there was no way Sabrina could have sabotaged Sally's if she was cooing over her nephew in another state.

Chapter Eight

Blackberry Valley
June 12, 1946

Blackberry Inn was the finest building in town as far as Sally was concerned, and working in the restaurant there made her feel proud. She loved the smart waitress uniforms, the gleam of the woodwork in the dining room, and the heavenly smells that came out of Betty Hill's kitchen. For the first time since Monsieur Antoine had abandoned her five years ago, Sally felt a renewed interest in food.

"I love people, so I give them a nice place to sleep and I cook them a good breakfast," Betty liked to say. "It's as simple as that."

Sally certainly felt loved when she ate Betty's applesauce muffins slathered with honey whipped butter. Or her buttermilk biscuits and sausage gravy. Or her chocolate pudding cake, offered to inn guests in the afternoon with coffee or tea.

Or, really, anytime she ate anything Betty made. Her food wasn't impressive or elegant the way Monsieur Antoine's had been, but it was undeniably good. When Sally first started waitressing and guests asked for recommendations, she inadvertently overwhelmed them by going through the menu item-by-item and describing why each one was delicious. Since then, she'd learned to limit herself to mentioning three menu items. Sometimes four. Occasionally five.

"Just had a request for your biscuit recipe," one of the waitresses said as she bustled through the kitchen.

"You know where to find it," Betty replied, the pan hissing as she added milk to the roux.

Sally, who was filling a basket with an assortment of muffins for a table full of women, watched her colleague flip through the stack of copied recipes, find the one that had been requested, and then carry it back out into the dining room. Customers asked for recipes so frequently that Betty kept copies on hand that the staff were invited to give to anyone who wanted one.

"Why do you share your recipes like that?" Sally asked, draping the towel over the muffins to keep them warm.

"Food is an expression of love," Betty said without turning around. "Love is best when it's shared."

"But these are *your* recipes," Sally said. "Don't you worry about what could happen?"

"What could happen? Sally, it's a recipe." Betty shut off the heat and tapped her whisk on the edge of the iron skillet. "My recipes are gifts from God. I don't want to clog up His goodness by hoarding my recipes all to myself."

Sally puzzled over this as she carried the basket of muffins out to the table along with a selection of spreads. She drank in the sight of the dining room. What would it be like to own a place like this, where tired travelers could sleep in comfortable rooms and enjoy a home-cooked breakfast?

She stepped aside to let a woman pass by with her young daughter. With one hand, the woman held her daughter's hand, and in the other, she held Betty's recipe.

"Will you make the biscuits when we get home, Mommy?" the girl asked.

"No, that would be a little soon." The mother smiled. "But maybe next weekend? Then it'll be just like eating at Blackberry Inn, only we'll be at home. Won't that be marvelous?"

Sally's lips pinched, and she shot an annoyed glare at the back of the woman's head. *This* was the problem. It ate into profits by allowing potential repeat customers to make what they wanted from the inn. Why couldn't Betty see it?

If she was ever fortunate enough to own a place as swell as this, she would *not* be sharing her recipes.

As Hannah went through the pantry to make notes on what needed to be restocked, her phone buzzed in her pocket. Her heart leaped with hope that it was Liam calling her back. All morning long, they'd been playing phone tag as both of them were in and out of meetings and conversations.

The phone call wasn't from Liam, but Amelia. Hannah pushed away her disappointment and answered with, "Hi, Amelia."

"Is this a bad time?"

"Not at all. Why?"

"You don't sound very happy."

Hannah winced. "Sorry, now is fine. What's going on?"

There was a double beep, and she pulled her phone away from her ear to discover that this time it was Liam calling. *Of course.* She inhaled deeply and reminded herself that she could call him back when she was off the phone. Nothing to get upset about.

"I've been thinking about all the wonderful people who have helped me with the opening of Sally's," Amelia said. "People like Neil and Lacy, you, and Jason and his wonderful team of contractors. I want to show my appreciation by inviting you to a thank-you brunch a week from Monday."

Hannah frowned at the bags of cornmeal as she straightened them. "Amelia, that sounds lovely, but isn't that your opening day?"

"That's why I chose it. I think it's a perfect way to start the day. And to test out any hiccups in the kitchen."

"Well," Hannah said slowly, "I guess that's a good way to view it."

Personally, she thought the idea sounded potentially overwhelming. Amelia's day would be busy enough with all the last-minute tasks to prepare for her first guests, but Hannah could also see the sense in the decision. Even though Sally's breakfast offerings were much more limited than a traditional restaurant's, having some practice was a good idea.

"You can even bring a friend, if you like," Amelia said. "Or a date, if you're seeing someone."

Hannah's mouth opened, but no sound came out at first. She would love to say, "Yes, I'm seeing Liam Berthold." But going on one date and attempting a second didn't classify as "seeing someone," did it?

Instead, she said, "Thank you. I'll let you know if I decide to invite someone."

"No need," Amelia said. "Simply bring a guest if you like. Either way, I'll see you at ten o'clock on the twenty-second?"

"I'll be there."

Hannah hung up and immediately called Liam back—only to have the call go straight to voicemail. She sighed and hung up without leaving a message. But a moment later, her phone alerted her to a new voicemail.

"Hi, Hannah." Just the sound of her name spoken in Liam's deep, rumbly voice made butterflies take flight in her stomach. "I'm heading to lunch with some others from the station and was hoping to catch you before going in. This is probably a long shot, but what about lunch after church on Sunday? I saw the empty spot on my calendar and hoped you might be free then too. If not, I'm sure we'll find another time. I'll talk to you later."

Hannah was glad she was alone, because her grin felt comically large as she texted Liam. SUNDAY LUNCH SOUNDS PERFECT.

Hannah tried to stop looking repeatedly at Liam during Pastor Bob's sermon. He sat several rows in front of her and off to her left. Even when she wasn't staring at him, she was keenly aware of him in her peripheral vision.

She felt a giddiness akin to childhood Christmas mornings as she anticipated their date. Since most area restaurants didn't open until noon, Liam had suggested that they take a walk on one of the area trails before getting lunch. Hannah had struggled to put together an outfit nice enough for church and a date but also comfortable enough for walking around on a trail.

When the service was over, she chatted first with Connie Sanchez, the church secretary, and then with Amelia, who beamed as she told Hannah about the deal she was getting on a commercial mixer.

"The downside is that Isaac had to drive to Louisville yesterday to pick it up, but it's worth it for the price. We're getting it for half of what they sell for new, and this one is only a year old." Amelia clapped her hands together as if Isaac had gone to pick up a puppy. "I'm so excited to see it when he gets back this afternoon."

Hannah grinned, remembering times when she'd been in raptures over a new espresso machine or the first copper pot she'd ever owned. "I'll have to come see it, though it'll probably make me jealous. And I'm glad you were able to get a deal. When I was opening the Hot Spot, it felt impossible to get anything for a commercial kitchen at a reasonable price."

Over Amelia's shoulder, Hannah saw Liam standing by the door. He was visiting with Neil, but she could tell that he was keeping an eye on her, gauging when she was ready to go. Her stomach gave a pleasant dip. They were *finally* going to have this second date.

A beeping sound invaded Hannah's conversation with Amelia.

"Oh, that's me." Amelia fumbled in her purse for her phone. "I left dough rising, and I knew I would get talking and forget all about it if I didn't set a timer." She silenced the alarm and then smiled at Hannah. "Nice to see you, Hannah. Hope you have a great day."

"You too, Amelia."

As soon as Amelia stepped away, Liam ended his conversation, and Hannah made her way over to him. She hoped her smile wasn't so big that it scared him.

"You ready to go?" he asked.

She felt her cheeks flushing. "I am."

He smiled and pulled the door open for her. "Then let's have this date."

Hannah had been in Liam's Jeep a few times, and it was always tidy, with the lingering masculine scent of his cologne or aftershave. She buckled herself into the passenger seat and forced herself to take deep, slow breaths as Liam made his way to the driver's side. She wasn't nervous, exactly, but it did feel like her heart was trying to break out of her rib cage.

"Pastor Bob was really fired up today, wasn't he?" Liam asked as he started the Jeep. "He has been this whole sermon series."

"I love it," Hannah said. "Seeing the enthusiasm of others about what God is doing or saying is always so encouraging."

"That's something he's really good at," Liam agreed. "I wish I could get my grandpa to come to church here. I think he'd get a lot of enjoyment out of the services, but he likes going at Clarkston Commons. And it makes sense. That's where his friends are."

"I understand that. I know church isn't meant to be a social club or anything, but I like being in the same faith community as Lacy and Amelia and many of my other friends. How's your grandfather feeling?"

"Better, he says. Sounds like the antibiotic is doing its job."

"I'm so glad to hear that." Hannah opened her mouth to ask another question about Patrick but was interrupted by her phone buzzing in her purse. She intended to push the call into voicemail but hesitated when she saw the name on the screen. Why would Amelia be calling when they'd just spoken?

"Sorry," Hannah said. "This is Amelia, and it seems like an odd time for her to call."

Liam smiled at her. "You should probably answer then," he said.

Hannah pressed the phone to her ear. "Hi, Amelia."

"Hannah, can you come to my place?" Amelia's voice had the characteristic tightness of restrained tears. Hannah hated that in her short time of knowing Amelia, she knew exactly how the older woman sounded when she'd been crying.

"Is something wrong?"

"Yes. I've—" A sob broke through. "Someone broke into the B&B."

Hannah gasped. "Amelia, are you all right?"

"Yes, but I can hardly believe it. I've called the police, and they're on their way, but Isaac is still in Louisville, and I don't want to be alone. Do you mind coming over and waiting with me?"

Liam must have been able to hear Amelia's side of the conversation, because he was already pulling over to turn around. They'd barely left the Blackberry Valley city limits.

"Of course not. I'll be there as quickly as I can, Amelia. Do you want to stay on the phone while I head that way?"

"Thank you, but no. I need to call Isaac."

"She should wait out front," Liam cut in. "Not inside."

Hannah passed that along.

"I'll head outside right now," Amelia confirmed.

"See you soon."

Hannah hung up and clutched her phone in her lap, as if doing so would help keep Amelia safe. "Thank you for turning around," she said. "I can't believe someone actually broke into Sally's."

"That poor woman." Liam shook his head. "Amelia is as sweet as they come, and it's been one obstacle after another for her. Did she say if they took anything?"

"I didn't even think to ask."

"We'll know soon enough."

Liam's mouth was set in a grim line, and Hannah felt the vehicle increase in speed. She wouldn't have dared drive so fast on this road, but of course Liam was the fire chief, and his blue Jeep was easy to recognize. If a police officer saw Liam speeding, they would know it was because he had a good reason.

"I'm sorry about our date," Hannah said quietly.

When he smiled at her, the corners of his eyes crinkled. "Me too."

"Maybe we'll still be able to have lunch."

"If not, we'll find another time. Right now, we'll see what kind of support Amelia needs."

Hannah's heart swelled. That was Liam. Others first, always. His prioritizing Amelia right now made her even more appreciative of their deepening relationship, as did his assurance that they would find another time if today didn't work out. The doubts that had been living in Hannah's heart—that the interest she felt in him might be one-sided—diminished.

When Liam pulled into the circular drive of the bed and breakfast, Amelia was pacing the length of the porch, arms crossed like she was trying to hold herself together. The relief on her face when she saw them chased away Hannah's lingering regrets about not being on her date. The best use of their time right now was taking care of Amelia.

"Thank you so much for coming over." Amelia was trembling when Hannah embraced her. "I can't believe this is happening."

Next, Amelia hugged Liam. Liam's years of being in first-response work meant that he was used to interacting with people who were shocked or afraid, and Hannah wasn't surprised to see that he hugged Amelia back.

"I'm so glad you called us," Liam said, his voice calm and authoritative. "Was anything stolen?"

Amelia fussed with the buttons of her cable-knit cardigan. "Everything from the safe in my room is gone. Cash, Mom's and Grandma's jewelry." Amelia's eyes filled with tears. "But worst of all is Mom's recipe box."

The words hit Hannah like a punch in the gut. Sally's secret recipes were secret no more.

Chapter Nine

Deputy Jacky Holt was the responding officer, and Hannah was grateful to see her. In her experience, Jacky was thorough and serious but also compassionate. After she walked through the entire bed and breakfast on her own to make sure nobody was inside, Jacky had Amelia accompany her to the safe. She allowed Hannah and Liam to tag along, and they silently wound through the kitchen and into Amelia's bedroom.

Amelia gestured toward her nightstand, which held only a lamp and a copy of *The Memoirs of Sherlock Holmes*. Hannah wondered if that was on Neil's recommendation. When he got excited about a series or an author, he tended to infect the whole town with his enthusiasm.

Above the nightstand, the safe door was open, revealing its empty insides.

Jacky pulled on gloves. "This isn't exactly a new safe, is it?"

"It's original to the property. My mom told me this room used to belong to a chef, and the safe was installed as part of his contract."

Jacky's eyebrows arched. "They had a chef who lived with them? Lucky."

"Only for a little while, I think. Mom didn't talk much about him, at least not until just before she passed away. Then she spoke as though he was the most influential person in her life." Amelia shook her head, as if clearing it to get back to the subject at hand. "Anyway. I think he was the only cook who ever lived at the house. Not many personal chefs want to live in a rural community, I guess. Eventually my grandparents hired local women to cook for them, but none of them lived in the house as far as I know."

Jacky eased the door of the safe to where it was nearly closed and then opened it again. "No sign of forced entry. Who has the combination?"

"Just me."

"Do you have it written down somewhere?"

Amelia hesitated. "Yes."

"And where is that?"

Amelia's gaze drifted to her nightstand, which was right under the safe. "In my nightstand drawer."

Jacky pulled out the drawer and raised an eyebrow at Amelia.

"I know," Amelia said with a groan. "I have it right on top."

"Well, at least you didn't write 'This is the combination to the safe in the wall above' on it."

Amelia gave a wry chuckle. "You're saying I have *some* brain cells."

"More than some. This could happen to anybody." Jacky turned on a small flashlight and inspected the inside of the safe. "And it's certainly not your fault that someone broke in here and took things that belonged to you. Tell me again what you kept in here?"

"About five hundred dollars in cash. Mom's and Grandma's wedding rings and several necklaces that belonged to my grandmother. I can show you photos of those." Amelia twisted her fingers together. "And a wooden box full of family recipes."

Jacky nodded along as she wrote this down. Then she turned away from the safe and looked around the room. "Is anything else missing?"

"Nothing from this floor. Not that I've noticed anyway." Amelia went back to fussing with the buttons of her sweater. "I didn't want to go upstairs by myself."

"Very wise," Jacky said. "I'd like for you to walk through with me to make sure nothing else is missing. Do you mind?"

"Of course not."

"Who all knows about the safe?" Jacky gestured to the wall. "It isn't hidden, of course, but most people don't have safes built into their bedroom wall. The fact that things like your television and your laptop are still here makes me think the burglar knew about the safe and targeted it."

"That makes sense," Amelia said. "It's not exactly a secret. Anybody who's been in the room for construction or for cleaning knows about it. Isaac, my nephew and business partner, knows about it, of course. Jason Perez, my general contractor. Although I think it was my original contractor, Adam Bristow, who did all the work in this room."

Hannah's heart beat a little faster. Not only had a shutoff valve started to leak on the same day that Adam had been seen walking around on the property, but now a safe that he'd known about and had access to during construction had been opened and emptied?

But why would he do it? The motivation behind taking cash was understandable, but family jewelry? If his plan was to sell or pawn the pieces, he'd have to go out of town to do so. And why take the recipe box? She remembered Adam making several jokes about being a terrible cook, which was great for Amelia's business but weakened him as a suspect.

But there *was* somebody who'd voiced an interest in those secret recipes.

"What about Violet?" Hannah asked. "Did she know about the safe?"

Amelia frowned. "I don't know. I don't think so."

"Who's Violet?" Jacky asked, pen poised above her notepad.

"Violet Presley. She was supposed to get married here on the property a week ago Saturday, but when the opening was delayed, I had to cancel her reservation." Amelia hesitated. "She didn't take it well."

"I was here when she threatened Amelia and Isaac both, saying she'd make them pay," Hannah added. "I also spoke to her last Wednesday at Jump Start. I asked her about the water leak, and she said she wouldn't have taken revenge like that. But she did say she would post your secret recipes if she knew where they were."

"But she couldn't have known where they were," Amelia protested. "I didn't say anything to her about where I keep them. And she's never been in this room."

"Whoa, whoa, whoa." Jacky held up a hand. "What leak are you talking about? Is this something you should have reported to the police?"

"I don't know," Amelia said, squirming under Jacky's sharp gaze. "For one thing, we were never completely sure it was a criminal act. What would I have said if I called? 'Hello, Officer, somebody might have messed with the shutoff valve in my bathroom to cause a leak? Or it could have been an accident?' It seemed silly to bother the police over something that might not have been anything."

"Amelia." Jacky gave her a look that was somehow both warm and exasperated at the same time. "This is my *job*. It's never a bother for us to come and check out something like that. Call us next time. We're here to help."

Amelia continued to wring her hands. "I should've listened to Isaac. He said he thought we should stop the remodel and delay the opening so the police could come in and take a look, but I'd already delayed the opening once." She gave a humorless laugh. "I should've bought Blackberry Inn from Sabrina when I had the chance. Then I would've been open months ago without any of this headache."

Hannah put an arm around Amelia's shoulders. "But your dream is Sally's, right here where your mom grew up. You couldn't have achieved that by purchasing Blackberry Inn."

Amelia nodded. "Yes, I know you're right. Thank you for reminding me. This is just so *hard*."

"I know it is." Hannah squeezed Amelia closer. "We'll help you get through it though. This will all be worth it in the end."

"I hope so, because it sure doesn't feel like it right now." Amelia cast a forlorn look at the empty safe. "Losing the money hurts, but I can make more money. Even the jewelry doesn't bother me too much. But the recipe box…" Amelia clenched her jaw, but still it trembled.

Hannah clearly remembered the stress of opening the Hot Spot, and she could only imagine how much more stressful it would have been if she'd been targeted the way Amelia was.

"Let's walk around the rest of the place, okay?" Jacky suggested. "You can point out anything that doesn't seem quite right. Then I'll get a kit and dust for prints. Most people are savvy enough to wear gloves, but every once in a while, we catch a break."

The four of them walked through the main level of Sally's, and while Hannah knew this wasn't meant to be a tour, she couldn't help marveling at how beautiful everything was.

Amelia explained that what was now the dining room had originally been a living room. The tables and chairs were all different from one another yet somehow went together. Creating such a look took a lot more time and energy than ordering matching pieces. There were high ceilings, and wide windows that overlooked the wooded backyard sprinkled with groupings of Adirondack chairs. The patio was lined with rocking chairs and small side tables, and Hannah thought when she came to eat here, that was where she'd want to enjoy her coffee.

"Is anything missing in here?" Jacky asked.

Amelia's gaze traveled around the room, and then she shook her head.

The group moved into what had once been used as a parlor. Hannah had barely noticed the space when they came in earlier, but the room had been transformed since she'd been there last. An L-shaped wooden standing desk perfectly matched the gleaming banister on the curving stairs, along with several chairs gathered around the tiled fireplace. Above the mantel hung a map of Blackberry Valley that Hannah was sure had been purchased from Legend and Key.

She couldn't help thinking of the longing in Sabrina's voice when she'd talked about remodeling Blackberry Inn. Sabrina would love to be able to spend the kind of money to overhaul her place that Amelia was spending here. Could jealousy have motivated Sabrina to steal from Amelia?

"Has Sabrina been in here?" she asked.

Amelia shook her head.

"Sabrina Hill?" Jacky asked.

Hannah wished she'd waited to ask Amelia in private. There was no reason to suspect that Sabrina was involved with the break-in. Hannah wouldn't have considered her, except for earlier conversations she'd had with Amelia about the water leak.

"With their similar businesses, I just wondered," Hannah said.

"Wondered if she'd broken in?" Jacky asked.

Hannah felt her face going red. For all she knew, Jacky and Sabrina were friends or even family. Connections like that were always likely in a small community like Blackberry Valley. "No, I thought Sabrina would have a unique appreciation of all the work Amelia has put in."

Hannah tried not to feel too uncomfortable as Jacky wrote something in her notepad. Probably *Hannah Prentiss rambles when she's nervous.*

"Nothing different in here," Amelia said. "Everything is as it should be."

Jacky gestured toward the entryway with her pen. "There's a lot of footprints through here."

Amelia nodded. "It's been impossible to keep everything clean with all the construction. I've given up. I figured I would wait and give the floors a good going-over right before opening day."

Still, Jacky turned on her flashlight so she could observe the markings made by all the shoes.

"Can you tell which are freshest?" Liam asked.

Jacky's mouth quirked up. "I wish."

The group headed upstairs, and Hannah put her hands in the pockets of her coat so she wouldn't run her hand along the banister. Not that she thought it was likely it held the answer to whoever had broken in, but not touching anything seemed like a good idea.

Liam leaned forward and said so only she could hear, "I have a childish urge to slide down this thing."

Hannah grinned at him over her shoulder. "Go ahead. I'll be right behind you."

The spark of mischief in his eyes made her knees feel wobbly.

The second and third floors held a total of eight bedrooms, each of which now had its own bathroom. Hannah marveled at how lovely and unique each room was while at the same time creating a cohesive whole. She felt more certain than ever that Amelia had made the right choice in remodeling Sally's, because nobody else in the world could have shown the old house such love and care.

As if reading her mind, Jacky said, "You've done a beautiful job with this place, Amelia. I can't imagine how challenging it must be to furnish."

"A lot of the pieces are original to the house," Amelia said. "When my mother sold it after her parents passed, nearly all the furniture went with the house. Mom kept a few pieces that meant a lot to her or that were useful for our family, but my father was in the Navy, and we moved a lot. We had no place for all this."

Liam gave a low whistle. "It's amazing that so much of it is still here."

"Fortunately, the couple was ready to downsize and had no desire to take the furniture with them, so they sold it back to Mom with the house." Amelia surveyed the room they were in, with lavender walls, a four-poster queen-size bed in cherrywood, and a matching dresser. "This was my mother's room when she was a girl, and it's the only one that she redid before her health declined. She loved everything about lavender. The color, the scent, the taste. Her lavender lemon pound cake?" Amelia covered her heart with her hand. "Incredible."

"Another secret recipe?" Jacky asked with a smile.

"Not that one, because it was given to her. The only secret recipes are the ones she created herself." Amelia looked around the room once more. "Nothing missing here either. It seems like they specifically wanted what was in the safe."

Jacky tucked her notebook into her pocket. "I agree. I'll get to work dusting for prints, and I'll go check around outside. Was the front door unlocked? How do you think the burglar might've gotten in?"

"I'm not in the habit of locking the front door," Amelia admitted. "Not with contractors coming in and out all the time. Plus, it's a bed and breakfast. I want people to be able to come in. I lock up at night, but otherwise not so much."

Jacky nodded. "If I were you, I would put a lock on your bedroom door."

Amelia sighed. "It's been on my to-do list forever, but it was never the top priority."

"That's changed after this," Liam said. "I can take care of it right now, actually."

Amelia blinked at him. "What? Chief Berthold, you don't need to do that."

He waved away her protest. "It's no trouble at all. I'll drive over to the hardware store and pick up what I need. It won't take long to install it."

Hannah's heart fluttered at Liam's display of kindness, even if it did mean they definitely wouldn't have their lunch date today.

"Something with a key," Jacky said. "Dead bolt too. If you want to go now, I can see that Hannah makes it home. She's on my way back to the station."

Liam nodded. "Agreed. I'll be back."

He glanced at Hannah, and his hand rested on her arm for a moment. The gesture and his expression both held an apology. An unnecessary one. She knew who he was, and it was a big reason she liked him so much.

She smiled up at him. "Thank you."

He returned her smile and then disappeared out the front door.

Chapter Ten

Blackberry Valley
September 17, 1964

When Sally pulled up to the house in Blackberry Valley, her throat squeezed with the pressure of restrained tears. Ever since the phone call last week, she'd cried more than she had in her entire life. She couldn't believe both her parents were now gone. Papa's death had come five years ago—shortly after Sally had married Timothy and became Mrs. Jacobsen—and now Mother was gone too.

Everyone kept saying it was good that Mother's death had happened so quickly, that the Lord had been gracious and kept her from suffering. Sally knew that was true but also wished there'd been more time. With Papa, she'd been able to make it back to say goodbye. With Mother, she wouldn't have had the chance even if she still lived in Kentucky.

Seeing the house in such a state—paint peeling, lawn more dandelions than grass, a shutter hanging loose on the second floor—stole Sally's breath away. Mother must have been in worse health than she'd let on in her letters and phone calls, because the Sarah Arterburn Sally knew would never have tolerated such dilapidation. What a blessing that Amelia and Timmy were home with Timothy, because Sally wasn't sure how safe the inside of the house would be. Besides, they'd already seen her cry plenty of tears. She didn't want her children, even if they were so young, to see her cry more.

And Sally did cry more when she entered the house. The pieces of furniture stood in the same places they had been her entire life, but even with the thick layer of dust she could see how sun-bleached the fabric was. How the rug was coming unraveled in the corners and the wide plank floors sagged in places.

In her mind's eye, she could easily see the beautiful home of her childhood, and this felt like another death. The house had been dying slowly, and Sally hadn't been there in time to save it. Timothy was a Navy man, and they'd already lived in three different places in their five years of marriage. With all the demands of packing and unpacking, in addition to the arrival of children, Sally hardly ever came home.

When Sally told her mother they'd been reassigned to the Bay Area in California, her mother had said, "You may as well be moving to the moon. I can't visit you out there."

And she hadn't.

Sally had traveled home once when Timmy was a few months old. Though the long train ride had been brutal, she was grateful she'd done it. That had been less than a year ago, and Mother seemed fine. The house had been declining steadily as her parents aged, and yes, she'd noticed that some repairs were needed, but it hadn't been quite this bad.

Sally's footsteps echoed as she traveled to her favorite room in the whole place—the kitchen. She had been told by the ladies of the church that when they'd arrived, the kitchen had been the only messy room. Mother's bowl of oatmeal had sat on the counter, with the spoon still in it. The oats, brown sugar, and butter were all sitting out, as was the saucepan she'd simmered milk in.

Sally frowned at the thought of her mother's final meal being run-of-the-mill oatmeal. The church ladies had wiped the kitchen clean, it appeared. Even though it had been so many years since he'd left, Sally still thought of this as Monsieur Antoine's kitchen, and the attached room as Monsieur Antoine's room. What was he doing these days? Had he ever gone back to France?

There was a pang in Sally's breastbone as she thought of the loud, caring French chef and how icy she'd been to him in his final days at the house. She was old enough now to understand that Blackberry Valley, Kentucky, didn't hold much opportunity for a chef of his caliber and that he could likely make more money and enjoy more exposure for his talent in a bigger city. There was no undoing a silly choice made at age eleven though. Not only had she outright ignored him before he moved out, but she'd also lost the shortbread recipe he'd left behind for her.

"Hello?" a man's voice called out. Likely Mr. Higson, the real estate agent. "Mrs. Jacobsen?"

Sally hastily dried her eyes and strode toward the front door. "Hello. Thank you for meeting me here."

Sally and Mr. Higson engaged in the kind of small talk Sally associated with small-town living. When did she graduate? Had she seen the new school on her way into town? Did she know this or that family?

Finally, they got back around to the issue of the house.

"They don't build them like this anymore," Mr. Higson said. "A little work is needed, of course, but she'll be a real beauty when she's done. You sure you want to sell it?"

Every fiber of Sally's being cried out *no*. She hated the idea of selling the house, but she and Timothy had been round and round about how they couldn't afford to keep it.

"Maybe we could think of it as an investment?" Sally had suggested. "We could use part of it as a boardinghouse, or a hotel, and I could cook." In a flash of excitement, she thought of the Hill family and Blackberry Inn. "We could convert the living room into a dining room, and I could serve breakfast in there. In the afternoons, we'd offer coffee and dessert. I'd make my chocolate tart and—"

"Honey." Timothy gave her the same expression he used when telling her they had to move again. "How would we do that with Amelia and Timmy and whoever else comes along? And what would I do? There isn't exactly a naval base in Blackberry Valley. I'm sorry. I really am."

She knew he was right, but it didn't make the decision any easier.

Sally looked around the house now, aware that Mr. Higson watched her. He'd probably meant his question to be rhetorical, a joke of sorts, but she could see so clearly everything she would do if she could keep it. If she could turn it into the kind of place she'd dreamed of as a sixteen-year-old girl working in Betty Hill's kitchen.

She saw how she would transform the living room into a large dining room. Light would spill through the windows, illuminating the steam as it rose from coffee cups and stacks of impossibly fluffy pancakes. She could line the back porch with rocking chairs, maybe sprinkle a few out in the grass.

She looked away. "Yes," she managed to say. "We'd like to sell."

The inn of her dreams would never exist.

While Jacky worked in Amelia's bedroom, Hannah and Amelia sat in the parlor.

It was the first time Hannah had been at Sally's that she hadn't been offered coffee and some kind of delicious treat, but it was also the first time she'd been there and seen Amelia sit. No dusting or tidying or wiping. She simply sat and stared into the unlit fireplace. Seeing her friend like this made Hannah feel unsettled, but it was also nice to feel like Amelia was comfortable enough to just *be* with her. That she didn't feel like she was hosting a guest.

"Jacky's really good at her job," Hannah said. "Hopefully she'll find something, and we can get all your things back."

Amelia nodded absently. "It was silly of me to keep the combination for the safe in my nightstand."

"You heard what Jacky said. This isn't your fault. The person to blame here is the one who broke in and took what didn't belong to them."

"You suspect Sabrina?"

Hannah uncrossed and recrossed her legs. "I don't really know. I thought of her because your place is so lovely and she might be jealous that you have the means to remodel when she doesn't. Incidentally, I agree with you about the Art Deco renovation she has planned for the inn. It really doesn't fit."

Amelia nodded. "She and Isaac would get along well. Ever heard of the Goldenrod Inn in Louisville?"

"Sabrina mentioned it, but I don't know much about it," Hannah said.

"My friend Carol owns it. It was built in the 1920s, and it's full of Art Deco charm. Carol is a few years older than me, and she's looking to retire, so she put it up for sale. Isaac wanted me to sell Mom's house to buy it, because he thinks it's much cooler than Sally's Bed and Breakfast. There's a coffeehouse next door he'd like to take over. He'd probably love Sabrina's plans for Blackberry Inn."

"Kids these days," Hannah said, hoping Amelia caught the joke. After all, Sabrina and Isaac were only a couple of years younger than Hannah.

Amelia offered a fleeting smile.

"Anyway," Hannah continued, "seeing all the work you've done and how beautiful it is made me wonder if Sabrina had seen it too and then felt jealous or angry. Maybe she got jealous enough that she just couldn't help herself from coming into your bedroom and stealing stuff from your safe."

Hannah was relieved to see Amelia's smile again, because she'd been joking about the stealing part.

"I'm just kidding," Hannah continued. "Even if she was jealous of the work you've done here, why would she steal from you?"

"You're right," Amelia said. "Her causing the water leak makes sense to me—or makes *more* sense to me, anyway—because she might be trying to show me how much of a money pit this place is so I'll want to buy her place instead."

"That does make more sense," Hannah agreed. "Although I learned she was out of town when the leak happened."

"There goes that idea then." Amelia peered at Hannah. "Were you questioning her because of me?"

"Yes," Hannah said with a sheepish laugh. "Sometimes I can't help myself from doing a little sleuthing."

Amelia chuckled, some of the usual light coming back into her eyes. "I understand the appeal. Neil Minyard talked me into buying a book of Sherlock Holmes short stories, and it definitely makes me want to play amateur detective."

Hannah looked left and right and then leaned forward. "What do you say we take a magnifying glass to all those footprints in the entryway and then try to match them up with people in town?" she said in a stage whisper.

Amelia laughed at Hannah's teasing. "You're a good friend, Hannah. I'm so grateful for you. And Chief Berthold running out to get me a lock for my door? He really is a sweet man."

Hannah's heart squeezed. "He is."

"Not bad looking either." Amelia winked.

Hannah felt herself blush. "True."

The distinct sound of gravel crunching beneath tires came through the window as Isaac's SUV pulled into the circular drive. Through the parlor window, Hannah saw sprays near the tire wells, as if Isaac had been off-roading, though Hannah had no idea where, as the mud looked more black than brown.

"Oh, good." Amelia pushed herself out of the armchair. "I'm so relieved he made it back while Jacky is still here. He'll probably think of questions that I didn't."

The vehicle had barely come to a stop when Isaac leaped out of the driver's seat and dashed up the porch, as if he hoped to catch the thief in action. The front door flew open. "Aunt Amelia?"

"I'm here," she called in a calm voice.

Isaac rushed to his aunt and hugged her. Hannah hadn't seen this side of Isaac before, and it was sweet. She felt a little awkward sitting there while they hugged.

"What a nightmare." Isaac gazed at his aunt with more tenderness than Hannah would have thought him capable. "I'm so sorry I wasn't here."

"It's not your fault, Isaac. We couldn't have known it was going to happen. How did everything go with buying the mixer?"

"Fine." Isaac released Amelia. "Everything was as it was described in the ad, so it was easy. The next time Jason and his crew are here, I'll see if they can help me get it into the kitchen."

"You got the extra bowl too?" Amelia asked.

"I got everything I went for." Isaac waved to his SUV. "And then some. There's a stretch of the road they're resurfacing, and you can see I brought some of that home with me."

"What a mess," Amelia said. "It's on your jeans too. You might have to take those to the cleaners to get it out."

"I'll take care of that later. Where are the police? I saw the car out front." For the first time since his arrival, Isaac looked her way. "Oh, hi, Hannah. Sorry, I didn't see you over there."

"I called Hannah after I discovered the break-in," Amelia said. "I didn't want to wait here for the police alone."

"Okay." Isaac's smile was tight. "I guess that makes sense. Because I was thinking how funny it is that once again something has happened and Hannah is here."

His smile was still in place, but there was something sharp in his gaze that made Hannah's spine stiffen.

"She's here because I called her." Amelia took her nephew's arm. "The officer is in my room."

She led him away, leaving Hannah stunned and unsure of what to do next. Was Isaac implying what she thought he was? He couldn't seriously suspect her, could he? What would her motivation be? Not that it mattered, because Amelia would never in a million years think that she was involved.

Hannah was still sitting there—alternating between worrying and deciding she shouldn't be worrying—when Lacy's truck pulled into the drive. She had no idea why Lacy was there on a Sunday afternoon, but it was a relief to have something to do. She walked out the front door while Lacy was still unbuckling her seat belt.

"Why aren't you on your date?" Lacy asked. She nodded at Jacky's car. "And why are the police here?"

Hannah gave Lacy a summary of what had happened before saying, "Liam left to buy a lock for Amelia's door, and Isaac just arrived from Louisville. He and Amelia are talking with Jacky now." She bit her lip. "Isaac acted like he thought it was strange that something else had happened and I was here."

Lacy gaped at her for a moment then let out a laugh. "Like he thinks you're involved somehow? He can't be serious."

"I don't know." Hannah found she was twisting her hands and made herself stop. "He made a comment about my being here for both events, but that's not accurate. Today, Amelia called me after she discovered the burglary and asked me to wait with her until the police came. With the water leak, yes, I was—"

Lacy held up a hand to stop her. "Surely you know that you don't need to explain this to me. I know you didn't do anything, Hannah. So does Amelia."

Hannah clamped her mouth shut and took a deep breath before she spoke again. "Of course I know you all know that. But it really rattled me when he said it."

"He doesn't know you," Lacy assured her. "Nobody who does could ever think you were involved. What possible motivation would you have? It's ridiculous."

Hannah exhaled. "What are you doing here, by the way? Is Amelia getting her eggs from you too?"

"Legend and Key delivery, actually." Lacy popped open the back door of her truck. "Wouldn't fit in Neil's car, and I needed to run to the grocery store anyway."

"Need help carrying it inside?"

"You can get the doors for me." Lacy slid the large, narrow box from the truck. "If you're here and Liam is off purchasing a new lock, I assume your date is getting postponed again?"

"Yeah," Hannah said, unable to keep the disappointment out of her voice. "But how sweet is it that he offered to replace Amelia's lock today? That's a worthwhile trade."

In the entryway, Lacy set the box against the wall. She cast her gaze about the floor. "Lots of footprints."

"Too many," Hannah said. "Amelia said it's been impossible to keep the floor clean, so she gave up for the time being."

Lacy glanced around the room, as if she might spot something noteworthy. "Do we know how the robber got in?"

"Well, Nancy Drew, we're pretty sure they walked in the front door. Amelia doesn't keep it locked."

Lacy grinned at her. "Poke fun at me all you want. You know you'd be doing the same thing if you just arrived on the scene."

Hannah laughed. "You're not wrong. And Amelia is reading a Sherlock Holmes collection right now, so she gets it."

Lacy shook her head, but she was smiling. "Neil's doing, I assume. You know how he is when he gets in these phases." She gave an exaggerated look around the room. "So, what do we think, Sherlock? Is it Adam, since he would know about the safe and had the expertise to pull off the leaky pipe?"

Hannah frowned. "But why would he have stolen from Amelia? He's not broke, and he doesn't strike me as a jewelry guy or someone who cares about recipes."

"That's true. But we know Sabrina was out of town for the leak, so it can't be her."

"There could be two people involved," Hannah suggested, though she could hear in her own voice that she didn't believe it. "Maybe the leak and the robbery aren't related."

"It's possible, I guess," Lacy said. "What about the vengeful bride you mentioned to me?"

"Violet? Yeah," Hannah mused. "I think she seems the most likely."

"Did you say Violet?" Lacy asked. "As in Violet *Presley*?"

"Yes," Hannah said. "Do you know her?"

"I do, but not very well. Remember when I was driving to Glasgow for spin class? She was there too, trying to get in shape for her wedding or something. But what's even stranger is I just saw her on Main Street. I was at the bookstore picking up the map, and do you know what she was doing?"

Hannah shook her head.

"Shopping. And not casually either. I've never seen a woman so loaded down with shopping bags. It looked like she'd cleaned out that new clothing store." Lacy's eyebrows arched. "The timing of her being flush with cash seems a little coincidental, don't you think?"

Hannah's throat went dry. "Yes, I do. I think Jacky will be very interested to hear about that."

Chapter Eleven

Jacky nodded along to the information from Lacy as she wrote it in her notepad. "Violet Presley was already on my list of people to talk to, but this is helpful to know. Thank you. I'll be in touch." She said goodbye to Amelia and Isaac and strode purposefully to her car.

Isaac closed the door behind her then said to Amelia, "I hope she starts investigating this today. We can't open the bed and breakfast if we're having these kinds of issues."

Amelia replied with a somber nod. "I know."

Isaac's gaze landed on Hannah. "I'm sorry about earlier, Hannah. Obviously, I know you're not involved with any of this."

Hannah opened her mouth to reply, but Amelia beat her to it. "Yes, about that. Isaac, why in the world would you accuse Hannah of stealing from me?"

"I didn't mean it," Isaac said. "I was feeling stressed in the moment."

Amelia's fists landed on her hips. "What level of stress would you have to be at to think Hannah is anything but a friend to us?"

Isaac held up both hands. "I know, I know. With everything that's been happening around here, I've let the pressure get to me. I'm afraid I'm not as even-tempered as you, Aunt Amelia."

"I understand," Hannah added. "After all, it wasn't that long ago that I was renovating the old fire station and starting a new business. Doing one of those things is stressful enough, but when you're doing both at the same time, it can really wear on you."

"This is true," Lacy said with a wink at Hannah. "Believe me, this woman was an absolute nightmare to be around during the renovation."

"Hey, thanks," Hannah said.

Lacy laughed. "I'm teasing. Hannah was her usual delightful self, just more tired. And a little cranky sometimes. She was a tired, sometimes cranky, but still delightful Hannah."

Hannah snorted. "Don't help me." She gestured to the map Lacy had brought over. "I love this, Amelia. Where's it going?"

"Right here in the lobby." Amelia smiled at Lacy. "You're so thoughtful to deliver that today."

"My pleasure. Sorry to intrude on what's already a hectic afternoon."

Amelia waved away Lacy's words. "No need to apologize. And you brought helpful information with you about Violet." She shook her head. "I wish I'd never booked that wedding."

Isaac rested a hand on his aunt's shoulder. "We're learning as we go."

"Thank you for waiting with me until Deputy Holt came," Amelia said as she folded Hannah into a hug. "You're such a good friend."

"I was happy I could help," Hannah said as she and Lacy were nearly ready to head out. "Let me know if you need anything else. I'm praying for you both," she added to Amelia and Isaac. She'd never seen Isaac at church with Amelia, so hopefully he didn't scoff at the idea.

But he nodded and smiled. "Thank you, Hannah. We need it."

Hannah was up to her eyeballs in receipts when her cell phone buzzed with Liam's call.

"Am I interrupting something?" he asked.

"Only bills and paperwork, so thank you." Hannah leaned back from her laptop, where she had her accounting software open. Her eyes burned from staring at the screen so long. She had no idea what time it was. "Did you just finish up at Amelia's?"

"Yeah, I had to drive to two different stores to find everything I needed, and then I had to borrow a tool from Archer to get the lock installed."

"You're a good man, Liam Berthold," Hannah said, warmth fluttering in her chest. "That's what my phone should say when you call."

"You're right," Liam said, a hint of teasing in his voice. "I do wish we'd gotten to our other plans today though."

"Yeah, me too." Hannah clicked over to her calendar. "Are you free December twenty-second for brunch at Sally's? That's the day the B&B opens, and Amelia is having a bunch of people over who have helped along the way."

"Sounds great, but please tell me I don't have to wait until then to go on another date with you."

Hannah felt those butterflies again. "I hope not, but I thought I better get that one on the calendar with all the trouble we've been having."

"This is one of the reasons I haven't dated much," Liam said. "It's hard to find the time."

"Yeah, same," Hannah said. "And I've always worked a lot of evenings and weekends. That's not ideal for dating either."

"You're often free on Sundays though, right? What if we go ahead and plan for a week from today? Like a date rain check. If we can find another time this week to see each other, great. If not, we'll still have that to look forward to."

Hannah's breath caught in her chest. "Yes. That sounds like a great idea."

They talked on the phone for so long that Hannah eventually saved her progress in her accounting software and powered down her computer for the night. Their conversation meandered from people they knew in high school, to the best meals they'd ever eaten, to places they hoped to travel and hobbies they would engage with more if there were additional hours in the day.

Hannah admitted to herself that she *really* liked him as she switched off the lights in her office and headed up to her apartment. She knew from experience that once they started spending more time together, the sheen of the new relationship would wear off. That could reveal problems that weren't obvious now, but that didn't necessarily mean the end of the relationship. She'd observed with Lacy and Neil, her brother and sister-in-law, and her own parents that a couple could disagree and still love each other deeply. A relationship could work—*should* work—after the newness had worn off. That simply hadn't been her experience yet.

But maybe it was about to be.

Chapter Twelve

Blackberry Valley
July 15, 1966

Sally thought the only blessing of having to return to Blackberry Valley, to her childhood home, was that this time she could bring Amelia with her. The Arterburn house had been for sale for so long—nearly two years now—that she had begun to despair that anyone would ever buy it. Apparently, there wasn't much demand in Blackberry Valley for nine-bedroom houses.

But finally, the place had sold to a couple from Louisville. Apparently, they had always wanted to live in the country and needed lots of space for their grown children and their families to come stay with them.

When Mr. Higson had called with the good news, Sally experienced a whirl of feelings. There was relief, of course. With their third child on the way, money was tighter than ever. The sale of Mother and Papa's house would go a long way toward financial stability for her and Timothy. No longer would she have to spend time lining up yard care or house cleaners or repairmen for any number of issues that popped up when a person owned a house across the country from where she actually lived.

So, yes, Sally felt relief. But the relief came with an aftertaste of sadness, regret, and a hint of bitterness. The grand house would no longer be hers. Her dream of transforming it into a remarkable place like Blackberry Inn was officially dead.

Timothy's mother had been happy to keep *either* Amelia or Timmy, but not both. So this time when Sally rode the train to Blackberry Valley, it was with five-year-old Amelia beside her. Sally was amazed by how easy it felt to care for Amelia by herself when compared to the task of caring for Amelia and Timmy at the same time. Her hand rested on the swell of her belly. Caring for children wasn't going to get easier anytime soon.

Mr. Higson was kind enough to pick up Sally and Amelia from the train station and take them to his office to sign papers. The town of Blackberry Valley had grown in the last couple of years, and it creeped ever closer to her parents' land. In another decade, the house might even be a part of the town.

Not that Sally would be back to see it happen. An ache crept into her throat.

"Do you mind stopping by the house first?" she asked Mr. Higson when they were a few blocks away. "I'd like to see the place one more time."

If he thought her desire was sentimental nonsense, he didn't say so. "Certainly, Mrs. Jacobsen. It's still your house."

Not for long though. The thought made something sharp form in her chest.

The sight of the house brought a wave of sadness mixed with shame. The meager amount of cash she and Timothy had been able to throw at the place hadn't done enough to keep it from sliding further into disrepair. She was amazed that anyone had looked twice at the place, much less bought it.

"What are we doing, Mama?" Amelia asked as they got out of the car. Her auburn curls were a mess after a day of travel, and her dress was full of creases.

"This is the house I grew up in," Sally said, gazing up at the window that used to be hers. "I'd like to go inside and say goodbye."

"To the house?" Young Amelia had already lived in several different places. The idea of being emotionally attached to a house probably didn't make much sense to her.

"Do you remember coming here once before?" Sally asked. "To visit Grandma?"

"Yes," Amelia said, but the expression on her face made Sally suspect that her daughter was giving her the answer she thought her mother wanted rather than the truth. "It's very broken."

"Yes." Sally's heart throbbed. "Hopefully the new family can take better care of it."

After telling Mr. Higson they wouldn't be long, Sally took Amelia by the hand, and together they walked up the sagging porch.

When Sally twisted her key in the lock and pushed the door open, Amelia slid behind her. "I don't think I want to go inside. It's dark."

"You can stay right with me," Sally said. "And everything will look nicer once I've opened a few curtains."

She felt Amelia grasp handfuls of her skirt and couldn't stop a small smile. Inside smelled of must and furniture polish. She opened the curtains in the living room, revealing dust motes in their silent airborne dance.

"It looks like somebody still lives here," Amelia whispered.

Sally wanted to get her child's mind off the unsettling idea. "Do you want to see where I learned to cook?"

"Yes, please!" Amelia trotted along beside her as Sally navigated through the living room and into the kitchen.

Amelia gasped in the doorway. "It's *enormous*."

Sally smiled. Amelia had recently learned the word *enormous*, and it was amusing to hear her apply it to everything from the number of brussels sprouts Sally had scooped onto her plate to the length of the train ride, and now to the kitchen. Though compared to the galley kitchen in their Navy housing, Amelia's assessment was accurate.

"When I was a girl, we had a chef," Sally said. "He was wonderful. Loud. Quirky. Made absolutely divine food."

"What's a chef?" Amelia asked.

"Someone who cooks for a living."

"Like you?"

"No," Sally said with a grin. "What I do is part of being a mother. A chef is different. That's someone who is hired to cook. He taught me everything I know about cooking."

She opened her mouth to tell her daughter more about Monsieur Antoine, but the words caught in her throat. He'd taught her so much simply by letting her be there in the kitchen with him, and she'd been too young and foolish to thank him. She thought of the recipe card he'd left behind for her. *Shortbread for Sally.* That she had no idea what had happened to the one recipe he'd written down for her seemed like a betrayal.

"Will you teach me to cook?" Amelia asked.

Sally subtly wiped away the tears that had welled and smiled at her daughter. "Someday, yes. I'll teach you the way he taught me, where you're right in the kitchen with me. That's the best way to learn."

"Will you teach me all your recipes?" Amelia asked. "Even the secret ones?"

Sally smiled even bigger. "Yes."

She thought of Monsieur Antoine and his secret recipes. So many of his habits had followed her into her own kitchen. The flourish with which she slashed her baguettes, her tendency to make tarts rather than pies—the list went on and on. There were probably things she did because of him that she didn't even realize. Such was the power of learning alongside.

"I want to learn how to make everything exactly like you." Amelia released Sally's hand to showcase her delight by twirling in the kitchen.

For a moment, Sally could see how life might have unfolded if she and Timothy could have kept the house. Amelia learning at her side while Sally cooked for their guests. The dining room full of small round tables instead of tired old furniture. She closed her eyes, let herself cling to the image for one more painful moment, and then let the dream go. It wasn't going to happen. Not now. Not ever.

"Do you want to see my room from when I was your age?"

"Yes!"

The curving staircase creaked more than Sally remembered, but none of the stairs sank when she placed her foot on them. She hadn't expected the sight of her childhood bedroom to take her breath away, but it did. The space hadn't changed at all since she was a girl. The white duvet with scalloped edging. The gauzy curtains that were pretty but did nothing to keep out the morning light. The cherrywood furnishings.

"This was your room?" Amelia asked. "It's enormous."

Amelia shared a room with her brother in their two-bedroom Navy housing, and once again her daughter's new vocabulary word was used well. This room *was* enormous, and Sally hadn't realized it enough to appreciate it when she'd grown up here.

The only thing out of place was a piece of paper on the dresser that Sally couldn't identify. She took several steps closer.

"What is it, Mama?" Amelia asked.

Sally wanted to respond, but her throat was clogged with tears and no words would come out. Written on the scrap of paper was "Found this behind the dresser and wasn't sure if you wanted it." Beneath it was a recipe card, the one she'd assumed was gone forever. *Shortbread for Sally.*

On the occasions that Hannah overlooked ordering an ingredient, it was always something basic. Flour, sugar, or—this time—salt. At least she could simply run to the market and grab a couple of boxes without breaking the bank. Still, it annoyed her when she remembered the ingredients for their seasonally special dishes but forgot something obvious like salt.

When she emerged from the market with her arms full of kosher salt and humming "Silver Bells," which had been playing inside the store, she found Isaac outside. He was crouched on the sidewalk, scratching Smoky, the fire department dog who wandered the town. Smoky's tail wagged and his tongue lolled out as Isaac scratched his neck.

Isaac caught her eye and smiled. "Hey, Hannah. Good sale on salt?"

Hannah laughed. "No, but we're low, and we blow through a bunch of it this time of year with brining pork chops." She nodded to Smoky, whose leash was looped around the bench. One of the firemen must be inside the market. "He looks happy."

Isaac's voice turned mushy in a way that seemed ill-fitting on him. "That's because he's such a good dog. Aren't you, Smoky? Aren't you a good dog?"

Smoky wriggled with delight.

"I've always gotten along well with dogs," Isaac said. "Sometimes I'm better with dogs than I am with people." He grimaced. "As you witnessed on Sunday when you came over to help my aunt and I accused you of being suspicious. Sorry about that again."

"We do things like that when we're stressed," Hannah said. "Don't worry about it. Any updates from Officer Holt?"

"Not that I know of." Isaac frowned. "I hope the police are taking this seriously."

"I'm sure they are," Hannah said.

Isaac avoided her gaze. "It's a small town, and my aunt and I are outsiders. I know we may not get priority."

"Nobody thinks of you as outsiders," Hannah said.

Although the truth was nobody thought of *Amelia* as an outsider. She'd lived there for the better part of a year, first as she cared for Sally in her final months, and then as she began renovating the old house. That didn't leave her with a lot of time to be involved with town groups or activities, but she still tried.

Isaac, however, was a different story. He'd only been living there for a couple of months, and he didn't come across as interested in being part of Blackberry Valley. In a lot of ways, he reminded Hannah of Sabrina Hill, who seemed to pride herself on being separate from the community.

Hannah wasn't at all opposed to life outside of their little town—she'd been away for over ten years before returning—but she didn't wear it like a badge of honor. To her, Los Angeles was no better or worse than Blackberry Valley. They were different places that were right for her at different seasons.

Hannah shifted the boxes of salt so she could give Smoky a pat as well. "Jacky's great. I'm sure she's working on it and hasn't had a chance to update you yet."

"Maybe." Isaac scratched Smoky behind the ears. "It's been two days though. We gave Jacky a list of everyone who's worked on the B&B in the last few months, and it was a pretty long list to get through, I suppose. It just feels like we should know more by now."

Hannah knew Jacky was capable of doing her job, but she wouldn't mind getting a look at that list as well.

"Hopefully soon." Hannah studied Isaac for a moment. She needed to get back to the Hot Spot, but she'd never really had a chance to talk to him away from Amelia. "Where did you live before Blackberry Valley?"

"Nashville. I was in a similar business to you, actually. I had a food truck."

"Really? Food trucks are fascinating. What kind did you have?"

"Grilled cheese truck called Cheese Please. I loved it." Isaac glanced up at Hannah. "I don't have to tell you how hard the restaurant biz is. I mean, it's one thing if you're the only show in a town like Blackberry Valley. It's another if you're one of thousands in a place like Nashville."

Hannah chose to ignore the dig at her restaurant's success. "Sure. It's really hard."

"I'd hoped to grow Cheese Please into a restaurant, but instead I grew the place into a mounting pile of debt."

"I'm so sorry," Hannah said. "I saw that happen so many times in Los Angeles."

"I wish that made me feel better. Fortunately, Aunt Amelia called and invited me to help with Sally's. I'm grateful to her for that. I know she's hoping I'll stick around, but..." Isaac cast his gaze along the street. "I don't see myself here long term."

"I used to feel that way too," Hannah said. "You think you'll go back to Nashville?"

Isaac shrugged. "There or maybe Louisville. I'd like another shot at a place of my own. A coffeehouse this time."

"Ooh," Hannah said. "I love a good coffeehouse."

"Can't happen here though. Not with Jump Start." He shrugged again. "I don't know. Hopefully working alongside Aunt Amelia on

Sally's can both help her and help me with my dreams of creating something special."

Hannah nodded. She could understand that. The reason the Hot Spot existed was that she had grown tired of working hard to make other people's restaurant dreams come true and had longed for a place of her own.

And yet she couldn't help feeling a bit protective of her friend. "Amelia knows this, I assume?"

"Oh, yeah. I was completely honest with her. She's hoping I'll stay, but she also knows that I don't intend to. Not for any prolonged period, anyway." Isaac glanced at his watch. "I better take care of my shopping, or Aunt Amelia will send the police looking for me."

Hannah smiled. "We can't have that. Good seeing you."

"You too," Isaac said. He gave Smoky one last pat and then strolled toward the market.

Hannah continued back to the Hot Spot. Despite the chill in the air, there were more people out and about than on a typical Tuesday evening. Many appeared to be shopping for Christmas or taking care of the extra to-dos that popped up this time of year. With the warm glow of the town's Christmas decorations, the scene was enchanting.

And yet Hannah's thoughts were on the theft at Sally's. She'd always felt so safe in Blackberry Valley, and the idea that someone among them was actively trying to harm her friend was nauseating. Why would anyone want to hurt a person like Amelia, who was doing something that would add value to their community?

When Hannah reached the Hot Spot, she found Sabrina sitting on a bench outside the restaurant, despite the cold. She wore her coat zipped to her chin and her hat pulled down over her ears. As Hannah was puzzling out why Sabrina would choose to sit out there, Togo jumped to his feet and started barking. Sabrina tugged at the leash in a vain attempt to silence him and gave Hannah an apologetic look.

Hannah laughed. "He takes his job of protecting you very seriously."

Sabrina smiled, though Hannah wasn't convinced the young woman had heard her above Togo's barking. Since Sabrina didn't flag her down, Hannah assumed she wasn't waiting to speak with her and proceeded into the Hot Spot.

Inside, Elaine was returning to her hostess stand after showing a group to their table, and she smiled at Hannah. "Did you leave salt for anybody else in Blackberry Valley?"

"There's plenty if they want table salt." Hannah jerked her head toward Sabrina. "She's not going to eat out there, is she? It's forty degrees tonight."

Elaine shook her head. "She's waiting for a takeout order. I told Jacob to put a rush on it because everybody who walks by or comes inside is getting an earful from that dog. I'm so glad Banjo doesn't act like that." Elaine's phone must have buzzed, because she pulled it from her waist apron and glanced at the screen. "Of course. I've been trying to get ahold of my cousin about Christmas dinner plans, and *now* she calls."

"You take the call, and I'll fill in for you here."

Elaine hesitated. "Are you sure?"

"Positive. Can you take the salt to Jacob on your way?"

Elaine took the boxes and said, "I'll be back in a few minutes. Thanks so much, Hannah."

Hannah stood at the hostess stand, straightening menus and keeping an eye on the people as they walked by outside. Togo was an excellent alarm for when someone was coming along the sidewalk. When a call came in for a takeout order, Hannah had to plug her free ear so she could hear, because Togo was going ballistic as Colt walked Smoky back to the firehouse. Not until Hannah had submitted the takeout order and hung up did Togo stop barking and sit down at Sabrina's feet once more.

But it wasn't more than a minute before Togo leaped to his feet once again, barked twice, and then, surprisingly, stopped. Hannah chuckled to herself to see that it was Isaac who was passing by. Sabrina smiled as he walked by her, apparently delighted to have found someone her dog wouldn't bark at, but if Isaac noticed, he didn't show it. He appeared oblivious to Sabrina and only glanced at Togo. The man might truly be better with dogs than he was with people.

"Here's that to-go order for the woman on the bench," Dylan said as he appeared at Hannah's side.

"I'll take it out to her," Hannah said, and he handed it to her. "Thanks."

Predictably, Togo started barking as soon as Hannah exited the restaurant.

Sabrina looked relieved. "Thank you. I'm so sorry about all the noise."

"It's okay," Hannah said, raising her voice to be heard above Togo as she handed the bag to Sabrina. "How are you?"

"I better go so I don't drive away business from your restaurant," Sabrina yelled, wrapping the leash around her hand. "Have a good night."

Before Hannah could figure out a way to get Sabrina to stay long enough to ask if she knew about what had happened at Sally's, Sabrina turned on her heel and walked away. That was probably for the best. Hannah clearly didn't have Isaac's gift with dogs, and Togo likely would have barked too loud and too long for her to get much information anyway.

She would have to find another way to talk to Sabrina.

Chapter Thirteen

When a takeout order came through later that night for an "Adam" who had ordered a Five Alarm Burger, Hannah found herself hoping the order was for Adam Bristow. She made sure to be the one to bring it out and was rewarded by the sight of him waiting at the counter.

Adam smiled at her, though it seemed strained. "Hey, Hannah. How's your night going?"

Hannah cocked her head to one side and studied him. There were circles under his eyes, and his smile lacked its usual warmth. Was he being eaten up with guilt over taking something that wasn't his?

"Better than yours, I'd guess. Are you doing okay?"

He shook his head. "I wish I'd never taken that job at Sally's. I spent hours being grilled by the police about the robbery over there. What a mess."

Hannah leaned against the counter. "Agreed. It doesn't seem like something that should happen around here."

He rubbed at the scruff of his chin. "Yeah, it's awful."

But there was something in his tone that made Hannah think he had more to say and was debating whether he should. She let the silence stretch, giving him plenty of space to finish his thought.

He cleared his throat. "Amelia's a sweet woman, but she also kept the code for the safe right there in her room. One time I saw a sticky note with four digits written on it sitting on her nightstand, which I assume was the combo. Now, I didn't break into her safe, and I never would, but if I'd wanted to, it would've been easy. And that's true for everybody who works there."

Hannah nodded along calmly, as if her heart weren't hammering in her chest as she considered what he said. That meant Adam likely knew the combination. While his words made it clear that he might not be the only one with that knowledge, that could be intentional. Maybe he was purposefully making it sound like of course he knew, but everybody who'd worked at the house might know.

"Did the police say what was stolen?" Hannah asked as she ran Adam's credit card.

"No." Adam drummed his fingers on the countertop. "I think that's intentional. They don't say what was stolen and hope that whoever they're interrogating slips up somewhere during the interview." He gave a sharp laugh. "That they'll say something like, 'What would I even do with a diamond necklace?' and then the police can pounce on that. 'We never said a diamond necklace was in the safe. You must be the thief.' Like we're in a Sherlock Holmes novel or something."

Had he mentioned Sherlock Holmes because the fictional detective was the first one people thought of? Or because he'd seen the book on Amelia's nightstand?

"But you didn't fall for that?" Hannah asked, smiling to show she was teasing. "Didn't mention the diamond necklace?"

Adam snorted. "First of all, I would never assume that I'm smarter than Jacky Holt. But also, as I told the police, I saw inside the safe once before. Amelia left it open, I assume by accident. There was normal stuff inside there—jewelry, cash."

"And what did you do when you saw it was open?" Hannah asked.

"What any decent person would do." Adam shrugged. "Closed it and carried on with my work, which is exactly what I told Jacky."

Well, that was clever of him. Now there was a plausible, innocent reason that his fingerprints would be on the safe.

But even if that was true, Hannah still couldn't work out what would motivate him to steal from Amelia. Adam causing the water leak made sense to her because it could reflect poorly on Jason, his competitor, but why would he go to the trouble to break into Amelia's safe? As far as Hannah could tell, Adam wasn't angry with Amelia for firing him. Maybe if he was desperate for cash, that could be an understandable motive, but she saw no evidence that he was struggling financially.

Or maybe, like the water leak, this was also about Jason. Maybe Adam thought the crime would be pinned on the current contractor or someone on his crew.

Hannah leaned on the counter and asked in a quiet voice, "Who do you think would do something like this to Amelia?"

Adam's eyes flicked up to Hannah, clear surprise in them. "Break into Amelia's safe? I have no idea. That's what I told the police too. Jason isn't stupid enough to steal from someone who hired him, but there are always a lot of people coming and going on a construction site. Good-hearted people like Amelia don't think about how much access those guys have. That leaves a big pool of possibilities."

Hannah could see the sense in this, though she imagined the police found it as unhelpful as she did. "That's a bit scary to think about."

Adam shrugged. "Just don't leave your combinations lying around, and you should be fine." He lifted the bag with his order. "Have a good night, Hannah."

"You too," Hannah said. "Enjoy your burger."

She felt slightly guilty for grilling one of her patrons, but if the information could get them closer to figuring out what happened at Amelia's, asking a few intrusive questions was worth it.

Since Lacy had better and more consistent access to Sabrina, Hannah texted her. Hey, I have a weird request.

The reply came almost immediately. Let me guess—it's something to do with the theft at Sally's.

Hannah grinned. How did you know?

I'm your best friend. It's my job to know. What do you need?

There was no point in beating around the bush, so Hannah laid it out for her friend. Since you're in regular contact with Sabrina, would you be willing to see if you can feel out the likelihood she was involved somehow?

You bet. I'll get back to you with what I find out, if anything.

Thanks. You're the best.

I know. Lacy added a winking emoji.

So now it was just Violet Hannah wanted to talk to. Not that she knew how to go about that. Hoping to bump into the young woman sometime when she happened to be in Blackberry Valley seemed unlikely. Hannah could try to find Violet's address in Cave City, but knocking on her front door was probably too aggressive for the situation.

The police are handling this, Hannah reminded herself as she wiped down the counter. She knew that Violet was on the list of people Jacky would question, same as Adam had been. Hannah didn't need to insert herself in the situation.

But still it bothered her, even as she returned to the kitchen to see how she could assist Jacob.

When Elaine popped her head into the kitchen a few minutes later and told Hannah, "Liam is here to pick up an order," it was a relief to have something more pleasant to think about than robbery and sabotage.

She tugged off her chef's coat and hung it by the door before going out to say hi. She found Liam standing by the door, handsome as ever in his uniform.

"We're short-staffed tonight, so we decided to do carryout." Liam leaned on the counter and grinned at her in a way that made her heart skip a beat. "I volunteered to pick up the order."

Hannah smiled back. "That was kind of you."

"The life of a firefighter is one of sacrifice." Liam winked then glanced around the Hot Spot. "Looks like a good night."

Hannah's gaze swept the dining room, which she would describe as being comfortably full. Nobody was waiting for a table currently, but nearly all the tables were occupied. "So far, yes. How late will you work tonight?"

He shrugged. "I'll be done after dinner. Did you see my text about getting coffee together Thursday morning?"

Hannah frowned. "Didn't I respond?"

"No."

She grabbed her phone. "Really? I thought I had. I have a dentist appointment at nine, but that's the only thing. Oh, look at that." She turned her phone to show Liam the screen. "I *did* write the text. I just didn't send it. I was in the middle of writing it when Dylan arrived." She made a show of pushing send. "Now I have responded."

Liam laughed. "I think I could do ten o'clock. I have a meeting at ten thirty, but a thirty-minute date is better than no date."

"My appointments are usually done relatively quickly, so I might be able to meet you earlier. Then it could be more like a forty-five-minute date."

Liam shrugged his broad shoulders. "All of that is an improvement on the five-minute date we had on Sunday."

"That's true." Hannah finished loading the orders for the firehouse into the bag and handed it over the counter. "Maybe soon we'll work our way up to an entire hour."

Liam's fingers brushed hers when he accepted the bag. "An entire hour? That would be amazing. If you wrap up early tonight, give me a call, okay?"

"I will."

Hannah watched Liam leave the restaurant and stroll along the sidewalk until he was out of sight. She felt an undercurrent of frustration with her untraditional hours. Not only that, but she'd done such a remarkable job of making her life full and vibrant, of not waiting around to get married before she started living a life she loved, that now when she'd met somebody she'd like to spend more time with, they were stuck with coffee dates that lasted less than an hour.

Hannah's phone buzzed with a text from Lacy. VIOLET. BLACKBERRY MARKET. PRODUCE. HURRY!

Hannah didn't hesitate. She grabbed her jacket from under the counter, told Elaine she'd be back soon, and took off for the market.

Hannah spent the short walk between the Hot Spot and Blackberry Market planning out what she was going to say—only to arrive and discover that Lacy was already on top of it. She found the two women standing by a display of pomegranates having an obviously warm conversation.

Lacy laughed hard at whatever Violet had just said. "My favorite was always when she would yell, 'We can do hard things!' during a steep hill. I still hear that in my head whenever I'm doing something challenging. Oh, Hannah!" Lacy turned bright, wide eyes to her, as if she was shocked to see Hannah in Blackberry Market. "What a surprise. Violet, this is my best friend, Hannah Prentiss. Hannah, this is Violet Presley. We used to take a spin class together."

Violet's smile thinned and cooled. "We've met, actually. Hi."

"Hi," Hannah replied. "Good to see you again."

"Mm," Violet said, the corners of her mouth tight.

In the lull of conversation, the chorus of "Santa Claus Is Coming to Town" could be heard clearly on the sound system. Hannah searched for something to say, but as she did so, Violet was already angling her cart in a different direction. If Hannah wanted to ask her any questions, she was pretty sure she'd have to follow her out of the produce section.

"Have either of you heard about what happened at Sally's?" Lacy blurted.

Hannah glanced at Violet, who was still turned as though about to leave but hadn't yet stepped away. Violet's mouth pressed into a line.

"Are you familiar with the new bed and breakfast going in?" Lacy asked her.

Violet seemed determined not to look at Hannah. "Yes. Very."

"Well, there was a robbery there," Lacy said in a hushed voice, as though it was secret news rather than something being discussed all over town. "Somebody broke in and stole from the owner."

Violet adjusted the strap of her purse. "That's too bad."

Was that really all she was going to say?

"I think it's terrible," Hannah said, trying to hide her annoyance with Violet's indifference. "I can't imagine why anybody would want to hurt Amelia in such a way."

Violet huffed. "Obviously stealing from others is wrong, but that woman and her son are making enemies fast in this town. When you do that, this kind of thing is bound to happen."

Hannah felt her eyebrows rise. "So you think they're getting what they deserve?"

Violet's lovely face was set in a scowl. "Maybe. And before you ask, no, it wasn't me. I had no idea that Amelia even had a safe. Which is exactly what I told the police when they asked me about it."

Hannah didn't know what to say to that.

Violet narrowed her eyes at Hannah. "You are so blinded by them. They're shrewd business people, especially the son—"

"Nephew," Hannah corrected her.

"—and that small-town charm is just an act."

"I disagree," Hannah said in a stiff voice. "Amelia is kind and hospitable and—"

Violet scoffed and stepped away. "Good to see you again, Lacy," she called over her shoulder. With a pointed glare at Hannah, she stalked out of Blackberry Market, abandoning her empty cart.

Lacy frowned at the market doors as they closed behind the angry woman. "Don't take this the wrong way, Hannah, but I think in the future I won't tell you if I have Violet trapped in a conversation."

Hannah sighed. "Yeah. That could've gone better."

Chapter Fourteen

Hannah couldn't put off doing her laundry any longer. She was in the midst of gathering and prioritizing when her phone began to ring. She considered ignoring it—she needed to get the washer started before heading to church to work on sorting and wrapping gifts—but when she saw Amelia's name flashing on the screen, she answered at once.

"Hi, Hannah," Amelia said, her tone sounding as tired and overwhelmed as Hannah felt.

"Hi." Hannah cradled the phone between her ear and shoulder so she could continue pulling out the clothes she needed to put through the washer first. "How are you?"

"I don't know," Amelia said with a humorless laugh. "I really don't. Deputy Holt was just here to talk to me and Isaac. She said they've interviewed every possibility we gave them—Jason, Adam, Violet, and Sabrina. Jason even provided a list of everybody who's been here in the last few weeks. And it all turned up nothing. It's just so frustrating."

Hannah sank onto her couch. It *was* frustrating. Somebody had broken into the safe, and so far, they were getting away with it. "I'm so sorry, Amelia."

"It isn't as if I *want* any of them to be guilty of stealing from me, but I really want to know who's doing this."

"Of course you do."

"And Deputy Holt said they've talked to the pawn shops in the area, but none of my mother's or grandmother's jewelry has shown up." Amelia loosed a long sigh. "I feel so discouraged."

"I believe it."

After a beat of silence, Amelia said in a watery voice, "Worst of all is losing my mother's recipes. Maybe it's silly, but it's like losing another part of her."

"That doesn't sound silly at all," Hannah reassured her. "A few years ago, I broke a necklace that my mother had given me, and I cried as hard as I did the day she died." Tears came to her eyes as she thought of that moment in her LA apartment, the heaviness of the despair.

"She entrusted those recipes to me," Amelia said, "and I've let her down."

"You have *not* let her down," Hannah said fiercely. "Sally would be blown away by all the work you've done these last few months. You're working so hard to turn the place into the bed and breakfast she dreamed of. She talked about nothing else in her final days, and you're making her dreams come true in such a remarkable way."

Amelia didn't respond immediately. Hannah glanced at the overflowing laundry basket and tried not to think of all the Christmas shopping she'd been planning to take care of after the meeting at the church.

"Are you coming this morning to help with the toy drive?" Hannah asked. "We could have lunch together afterward. We can even leave town, if you'd like to get away from Sally's for a bit."

"No thank you. That's a kind offer, but I have lots of things to take care of around here." Amelia sounded resigned. "I had hoped to help with the toy drive, but I haven't made it to a single meeting. I wanted to come today, but now I'm waiting for a delivery. So I decided to call and update you because you've been so wonderful about all of this. Will you ask the ladies for prayer this morning?"

"Of course." Hannah scraped together a mound of laundry that was probably too ambitious for a single load. "Are you sure you can't meet for lunch? Or could I bring you something? You sound so discouraged."

"I am. And it isn't as though I don't know what the root of the problem is." Amelia offered another tired laugh. "Not only am I skipping out on meaningful community service like the Christmas toy drive, but I'm missing personal quiet time too. I get bent out of shape when I don't have regular time with the Lord."

"That's true for all of us." Hannah hunted for something encouraging to say. "You're almost there, Amelia. On Monday, you'll be welcoming your first guests."

Amelia was silent at first. "You're right," she said finally. "Less than a week. I hadn't really stopped to think about that."

The lift in Amelia's voice encouraged Hannah to carry on. "You've certainly had your share of setbacks, but the place is incredible. You're going to be open before you know it."

"I will," Amelia said. "You're right."

"Just five more days, and then all you'll have on your plate is the breezy job of operating a business that's open twenty-four hours a day, seven days a week."

This time, Amelia's laugh came from her belly. "Thank you, Hannah. This was helpful. I think my delivery guy just tried to call me, so I'd better go."

"You're doing great," Hannah replied. "I'll talk to you later."

After they hung up, instead of carrying on with her laundry, Hannah sat immobile on the couch. She felt a restlessness in her heart over her conversation with Amelia, as though she should be doing *something* for her friend. And what else could she really do in this moment except pray?

Hannah bowed her head. "Lord, please help Amelia. Please help us to discern the truth of who is trying to hurt her." She searched for how to ask for what Amelia really, truly needed, but she was already speaking to the one who knew. "You know what she needs most. Please guide her in that direction."

Fortunately for Hannah, Lacy was also behind on Christmas shopping. The idea of going to Glasgow with her friend sounded much nicer than running around the county by herself. So Hannah was in much higher spirits when they left together after a morning of sorting the wrapped toys for delivery.

Most of the drive to the neighboring town was spent with Lacy sharing stories from the farm and all the work that needed to be done to prepare for the ice storm that was supposed to arrive the following evening. After listening to Lacy's list, Hannah was glad that the only prep work she'd had to do for her business was make sure she had salt for the sidewalks and a well-stocked pantry.

"I think we'll be glad we got our shopping done today," Lacy said. "Every prediction I'm hearing makes it sounds like we'll all be frozen in place for a few days."

At a stoplight, Hannah made a show of peering up at the cloudless blue sky. "You'd never know it right now."

"Ooh." Lacy pointed at a fast-food restaurant off to the right. "Will it offend your culinary-educated heart if we hit a drive-through? I planned to eat something before I left home for church, but I got distracted by Flower, Niblet, and Sprout."

Hannah put on her turn signal. "Baby goats *are* distracting. Although I guess they're more like adolescent goats these days, aren't they?"

Hannah placed an order for both of them because she was nearly always in the mood for a cheeseburger. She'd gone to culinary school with people who would turn up their noses at a fast-food joint, but Hannah still thought it was tough to beat a cheeseburger and fries when it came to comfort food.

After retrieving their order, Hannah pulled into a parking spot so they could divvy up the food before driving on to the first store. Her phone buzzed noisily from the cupholder with an incoming text.

Hannah blinked at the screen, sure she was reading it wrong. "It's from you."

Lacy leaned closer and read aloud, "'Sabrina says she was at the inn all morning on Sunday.' Yeah, I sent that this morning, before the toy drive meeting. Did it just now come through?"

"I guess so." Hannah unlocked her phone and checked the time stamp. "Yeah. Just now."

"That's weird." Lacy took her paper-wrapped burger out of the bag. "If I hadn't been doing farm chores all morning, I probably would've wondered why you never responded. But yeah, I talked to Sabrina, and that's what she said."

"Do you know if anybody can confirm that she's telling the truth?" Hannah asked, unwrapping her burger.

Lacy smirked. "I couldn't exactly ask to interview the staff, now could I? But we know she spoke to the police, and they've cleared her."

"Yeah, I guess you're right," Hannah said with a sigh. "I just wish we could get some answers for Amelia."

"For what it's worth, Sabrina also seemed confused about why Amelia would be targeted in the first place. She even said, 'I'm the only other hotel in town, so who else would consider her competition?' It's too incriminating a thing to say if you really are the one messing with shutoff valves and breaking into safes."

"Unless you're saying that to cover your tracks," Hannah said. "But I see what you mean. While I can make a case for Sabrina causing the leak, breaking into the safe would be a strange choice. Unless she's trying to wear Amelia down or intimidate her. Or get Sally's recipes, but what's she going to do with those? She can't start serving them at the inn without Sally finding out."

Lacy seemed to consider it. "You said this once before, but the leak and the break-in could be two different people. We keep trying to find a motive that fits one person, but maybe that's not right."

They ate in silence for a few minutes.

"I find her so inspiring," Hannah said.

"Amelia or Sabrina?"

Hannah chuckled. "Amelia, for the way she's sticking with Sally's even when it's tough. Maybe it's silly, but it makes me think of the struggle Liam and I are having with finding time for a date."

Lacy didn't laugh, for which Hannah was extremely grateful. Even to Hannah's ears, it seemed a little silly to compare Amelia's giant renovation project with her and Liam trying to find space on their calendars for time together.

"Remember when we were kids and we thought grown-ups could do whatever they wanted?" Lacy asked in a dreamy voice. "I miss those days."

"Hear, hear," Hannah agreed. "Liam and I have lunch plans for Sunday, and we're trying to have coffee tomorrow, but we're attempting to squeeze it in between my dentist appointment and his public safety meeting, so it's still not ideal. After that, the next date we have planned is that thank-you brunch Amelia is putting together."

Lacy chuckled. "I'm not sure that counts as a date. Everyone I talk to is going to be there."

"We're not picky at this point." Hannah dipped a fry into a diminishing pile of ketchup. "Hopefully, it'll be easier for us to find time together after Christmas."

"Ooh, and then it'll be your birthday." Lacy's eyes lit up. "How do you want to celebrate turning thirty-six?"

The fact that Hannah had given zero thought to her birthday being less than two weeks away seemed like a sign that she'd reached a new phase of life. She had vague childhood memories of her parents sometimes forgetting their exact age or acting indifferent about how they celebrated their birthdays, and that had been the oddest thing in the world to a girl who tracked her age not just by halves but by quarters. She wasn't simply eight years old, but eight and three-fourths, thank you very much.

Hannah took her time chewing as she thought. In truth, she wanted to spend her birthday on a date with Liam. The kind where he came and picked her up and neither of them needed to rush away to a meeting or an appointment. But seeing him on her birthday seemed like a big step toward him being her official boyfriend. She wasn't opposed to a serious relationship with Liam, but they'd only been on one real date so far. What would he think if she suggested they have dinner together on her birthday?

"I don't know," Hannah said, because it felt a little silly to admit that a real date with Liam was what she wanted most. Even to Lacy.

"Give it some thought, okay?" Lacy said. "Are you working, or taking the night off?"

"I haven't decided." Hannah reached for her phone. "I don't even know what day of the week my birthday falls on this year."

Lacy rolled her eyes. "Do you want to know my opinion?"

"Desperately," Hannah deadpanned.

"I think you should take the night off. How many times do you turn thirty-six?"

Hannah laughed. "Probably just once."

"It's a special day," Lacy insisted. "You should really celebrate it."

Thirty-six. She didn't feel old, but it was getting harder to ignore that at thirty-six, her mother had been unknowingly in her twilight years because she'd died in her fifties. While Hannah knew that was abnormally young, she also knew that a long life wasn't guaranteed to anyone.

"I think you're right," she said. "I promise to close the restaurant on my birthday. Thank you, Lacy."

Lacy's face brightened. "Isn't it great having such a wise best friend?"

Hannah tucked her phone away. "It's marvelous. I greatly appreciate your wisdom."

"Though I'm not sure you need to *close* the restaurant just because you're going to be gone. Surely your staff can..." Lacy stopped and smacked Hannah's arm. "Hey. Isn't your birthday on a Sunday this year? The Hot Spot is *already* closed on Sundays."

Hannah giggled, and a moment later, Lacy joined her.

Hannah sat through her dentist appointment the next day expecting some sort of delay that would mean she couldn't meet Liam on time. Surely the hygienist would be chatty, or the dentist would have a flat tire on his way into the office and fall behind on his appointments. But instead, Hannah's teeth were cleaned and pronounced cavity-free, and she walked out the door earlier than expected.

She called Liam as she rushed to her car. "You'll never believe this," she said when he answered, "but I'm on my way."

The rumbling sound of his laugh warmed Hannah down to her toes. "You'll never believe *this*, but I'm already at Jump Start on the off chance you were done early."

"We might have an entire forty-five minutes."

"I'll go ahead and order your coffee. What would you like?"

Hannah asked him to order her a peppermint mocha then hung up so she could focus on driving. Clouds hung low over the valley, and the morning was misty. This was probably the front edge of the winter storm they'd been warned about. Hannah thought the mist made the whole valley resemble a picture from a children's fairy-tale book, and she felt grateful in her soul to live there, even if it was currently seventy-five degrees and sunny in Los Angeles.

As she drove by Sally's, Hannah lifted up another prayer for Amelia—that the Lord would provide smooth waters for the few days between now and the opening. That He would foil the plans of those who were trying to harm her and bring their bad deeds into the light. That the items stolen from Amelia would be returned to her undamaged.

At Jump Start, Hannah pulled into the spot next to Liam's Jeep and hopped out. The mist had done a number on her hair, so she tried to tame it with her fingers before heading into the coffee shop. Liam sat at a table for two. When Hannah walked in, he was bent over his phone, and she took a moment to study him. This kind, handsome, godly man was sitting at a table, waiting for her, and the thought made warmth run up her spine.

He raised his head as she approached, and grinned broadly. "How are your teeth?"

She laughed as she took her seat across from him. "Very clean, thank you." She wrapped her hands around the coffee cup he had waiting for her. "It's chilly out."

Liam nodded toward the window. "Forecast says it'll keep getting colder as the day goes on, which could cause some problems with the roads freezing later this morning." He grimaced and drummed his fingers on the table. "Could be a busy day for us."

"I thought the possibility for ice didn't start until tomorrow."

"I'm just sharing what the email said. That's why I have a meeting at ten thirty, to go over the city's emergency plan."

"How funny. In your line of work, being busy typically means bad things are happening. In my line of work, a busy day is a good thing."

"That *is* funny," he agreed. "My busy days resulting from this storm might lead to some slow days for you at the Hot Spot."

Hannah hadn't thought about that. It sounded as if their struggle to schedule time together wasn't going to end anytime soon. "True."

Liam smiled and raised his coffee cup. "If the roads are going to get icy, I'm surprised it didn't happen right *before* our date. That's the way things have been going for us."

He winked, and Hannah laughed. "It really has felt like we're being conspired against."

As if on cue, her phone vibrated loudly on the table with an incoming text.

"Oh, please don't answer that," Liam said as she reached for her phone.

She laughed. "I'm not. I'm putting it away where it won't be such a distraction."

But as she picked it up, she saw the text was from an unsaved number. All she could read on her lockscreen was THIS IS ISAAC JACOBSEN. DO YOU KNOW WHERE...

Hannah bit her lip. Isaac was likely asking something innocuous like "Do you know where we should buy our beef?" or "Do you know where to have our linens laundered?" His message was certainly nothing she needed to look at right now when her time with Liam was so rare and precious.

"What is it?" Liam asked.

"Nothing," Hannah said, though the word curled into a question.

But if it was truly nothing important, why would Isaac text *her*? He'd never texted her before.

Regardless, if she didn't look at the entirety of Isaac's text, the question was going to occupy mental space and squeeze out her ability to focus on Liam. "I'm so sorry, but I need to check one thing."

Liam gave a small sigh but said nothing as Hannah unlocked the screen so she could read the full text: THIS IS ISAAC JACOBSEN. DO YOU KNOW WHERE MY AUNT IS? I CAN'T FIND HER.

Chapter Fifteen

For a moment, Hannah felt as though she was made of wood. Other than her eyes skimming over Isaac's words again and again, she was incapable of moving. Of feeling.

"Is something wrong?"

Liam's question broke her out of her shock. Worry ran through her, so warm she could feel herself start to sweat. "It's from Isaac Jacobsen, and I checked the message because it seemed like something would have to be very wrong for him to go to the trouble of finding my number and messaging me. Look what he's texted."

Liam angled Hannah's phone so he could read it, his fingers bumping against hers in a way that would normally make Hannah feel fluttery inside. But at the moment she felt too tense for butterflies.

"He can't find her?" Liam said with a frown. "That's strange."

Hannah turned the phone to where she could read the message again, as if the words might have changed. "I'm not sure how to respond."

"Probably with a phone call."

"Yeah," Hannah said with a groan. She tapped the phone icon next to Isaac's number. "I think you're right."

While waiting for the call to connect, Hannah locked eyes with Liam across the small table. He looked as discouraged as she felt. Was it really so much to ask that they have one date that didn't get interrupted?

Isaac answered with a crisp, "Isaac Jacobsen."

"Isaac, this is Hannah Prentiss. I just got your text. What's going on?"

"Do you know where she is?"

Hannah blinked at the abruptness of the question and the sharpness in Isaac's voice. "No, but—"

"When did you last talk to her?" Isaac's clipped syllables made Hannah's heart hammer in her chest.

"I spoke to her yesterday morning."

"What about? This is important, Hannah."

Liam must have been able to hear the bite in Isaac's voice, because he frowned at Hannah's phone as if that would do any good.

Hannah tried to reassure him with a small smile. "She told me about the update you guys got from the police and let me know she wasn't going to be at the toy drive yesterday morning."

"I need all the details. Where you were. What time of day this was. Everything you talked about."

"He needs to stop ordering you around," Liam said, a scowl on his face. "Ask him to tell you what's going on."

Hannah bit back a laugh at his expression. She'd had her fair share of being bossed around by people who had no business bossing her around, and she knew how to take care of herself. Even though she appreciated Liam's concern, she knew Isaac was stressed, and she wasn't taking his tone personally.

"Isaac," Hannah said as though he were a ruffled customer, "I'm happy to help, but first I need you to explain what's happened to Amelia."

"But I don't *know* what's happened." The clipped syllables elongated, but his voice remained tight with agitation. "When I woke up today, she wasn't here. Her car was gone. She wasn't answering her phone. It looked like she hadn't even been in the kitchen."

Hannah pressed her teeth into her lower lip and met Liam's eyes. His brow was creased. "But you saw her last night?"

There was a pause on Isaac's end of the conversation, and he blew out a long breath. "I saw that her light was on. We didn't have dinner together, which isn't unusual. I spoke with Jason this morning, and he had a text from her last night saying she would be away for a day or two and unreachable by phone. That if he needed something, he should talk to me."

The dread that had been knotting Hannah's stomach loosened at those words. "Well, that seems positive. This must be something she had planned—"

"But it makes no sense." Isaac's anger rose to the surface again. "We're a few short days from the opening. She said nothing to me about leaving for a day or two. This doesn't feel right to me."

Hannah had to agree that the timing *did* seem strange. In the days before she opened the Hot Spot, she certainly wouldn't have left town for even a day, nor would she have put herself in a position where she was unreachable. There had been too many things to do. But that might have been different if she'd had a partner. Amelia had Isaac. But why would Amelia have told Jason and not Isaac?

"Well," Hannah said slowly. "I agree. That does seem odd."

"I don't like that it was a text," Liam interjected, loud enough that Hannah was sure Isaac would be able to hear too. "A text could have been sent by anyone who has Amelia's phone."

"Who's that?" Isaac asked.

"I'm with Liam Berthold, the fire chief. I'm going to put you on speaker." She touched the icon and turned the screen toward Liam. "Did you hear what he said?"

"Yes. I hadn't considered that. But why would someone send a fake text from my aunt's phone? What would they gain from that?"

Liam shrugged. "I don't know. As strange as it may be to the three of us, someone around here doesn't want Sally's to open."

The relief that Hannah had been feeling when Isaac mentioned Amelia's text to Jason became a knot once again. Events *did* seem to be escalating in a way she didn't like. Each act against Amelia was feeling more and more personal.

"What time did Jason receive the text?" she asked. "Maybe it was so late or so early that she didn't want to wake him with a phone call."

"That's what I assumed," Isaac said. "Jason said it came in late last night. But what Chief Berthold said makes sense too, though I hate to think about what it might mean."

"Have you called the police?"

"We can't declare my aunt a missing person yet, considering she texted Jason that she would be gone for a couple of days, but I spoke with Deputy Holt, and she agreed that it was concerning and said they'd all keep an eye out for her."

"That's good to hear." Hannah cupped her free hand around her mug, soaking in the warmth.

"When you spoke to her yesterday, did she say anything to you about leaving town?" Isaac asked. "Maybe to pick up a purchase for the B&B, or visit a sick friend?"

"No, unfortunately," Hannah said with a sigh. "Like I said, she called to update me about the robbery. Let me think for a moment about what else we discussed." She closed her eyes and tried to go back to her apartment yesterday morning, with the laundry scattered all around her and the looming deadline of being at the church. "She told me the police had finished their interviews, but they really hadn't found anything. We talked about her sadness over losing the recipes and how stressed she felt, and how Sally's would be open in just a few days. I think that's all. I'm sorry I can't be more helpful."

"I appreciate it," Isaac said. "Please call me if you hear anything."

"Yes, of course," Hannah said. "Will you update me too?"

"Yes."

"I'll be praying."

With that, she ended the call and drew in a shaky breath as she met Liam's gaze. "I know it's possible that everything is completely fine, but something about it bothers me."

"Me too."

Hannah stared at her phone's black screen. "It's silly, but I think I should call Amelia."

"I don't think that's silly at all. What do you have to lose?"

Hannah pulled up Amelia's contact information, pressed her thumb on the screen, and prayed fervently while the call connected. Amelia's cheery but recorded voice said, "Hi, this is Amelia Jacobsen. Sorry I've missed your call." The message continued with Amelia providing the number to Sally's in case the person calling was interested in making a reservation, and telling them to ask for Isaac.

Fear raked over Hannah's heart as she waited for the beep to let her know she could begin her message. She tried to keep her voice upbeat as she said, "Hi, Amelia, it's Hannah. Isaac called to ask if I knew where you were, so I'm feeling a little worried right now. Call me when you get this, please."

She disconnected the call and placed the phone on the table between her and Liam. They both watched as the screen darkened. Hannah drew in a deep breath and looked out the window at the mist that was forecasted to turn into ice in just a few hours.

"I don't like this." Her voice emerged as an unintentional whisper.

Liam shook his head and stared out the window too. "Me neither."

Even after Liam left for his meeting, Hannah sat at the table in Jump Start, her mind spooling through the last few weeks in reverse. The emptied safe, the water leak, the canceled wedding, and the firing of Adam Bristow.

Surely Violet wasn't the only one who'd had a reservation canceled. Maybe there were others who were angry but hadn't been so vocal about it. Maybe they were smart enough to be slipping about unnoticed, intent on revenge.

Hannah grabbed her purse off the back of the chair and hustled out to her car. It felt as though she got behind every slow vehicle on the way to Sally's, but finally she arrived. The place wasn't full of construction vehicles the way it had been last week and the week before that. Now there was only a single van belonging to the painters. When she'd been renovating the Hot Spot, Hannah had been so relieved when the painters arrived because their presence signaled the end of the process. She wished Amelia was here to enjoy it.

But Amelia had gone somewhere intentionally, she reminded herself. She'd sent that text to Jason.

Or someone else had sent the text from Amelia's phone to defuse suspicion.

Hannah shivered at the unbidden thought as she parked her car behind the van. That was an idea Liam had suggested, not a fact.

She opened her door, stepped out into the drizzle, and tugged the zipper of her coat higher.

"You didn't need to come over."

Hannah turned toward the sound of Isaac's voice. He stood on the porch, his phone in his hand and his own jacket unzipped. She'd never seen him when he wasn't perfectly put together, and his unkempt appearance startled her. He still wore his usual trendy clothes—tailored pants, button-up shirt, and a coat that appeared more fashionable than warm. But his dark hair was loose from its typical gelled hold, and his face had a drawn expression, as though a few hours of Amelia's absence had aged him.

"I'm worried," Hannah said. "And I thought of something I wanted to ask you."

Isaac's eyebrows rose, and he nodded. "You don't need to stand out in the rain. Come on inside."

Gravel crunched beneath Hannah's shoes as she walked around to the porch steps. "I don't want to take up a lot of your time. I know you have a lot to do."

Isaac's laugh held no humor, and he raked a hand through his hair. No wonder the gel had all come loose. "I do. I wish my aunt had thought of it that way instead of dumping the whole to-do list on me."

"But she told Jason she'd be back in a day or two—"

Isaac released another mirthless laugh as he reached for the door handle. "That's about all we have until we open. Do you want coffee?"

"No, thank you. I'm not trying to interrupt—"

"You're not interrupting, and it's cold out here." Isaac's smile looked like an attempt to seem hospitable, but it came off as more of a grimace. "Let's talk inside."

The entryway and stairs had been covered with plastic, and Hannah could hear music and conversation coming from upstairs. The distinct smell of fresh paint mingled with the scent of coffee.

"That's better." Isaac closed the door behind her. "Ghastly weather. It's only supposed to get worse too."

Hannah pressed her hands deeper into her coat pockets. It *was* nice to be out of the damp chill. "That's what I hear."

"Which makes me even more nervous about Aunt Amelia. I don't understand why she wouldn't have told me where she was going."

That part worried Hannah too. "I don't understand that either."

"I know she's probably picking up supplies or something like that in Louisville, but why not tell me that? And why would she be unreachable, and for such a long time? What is she up to?" Again, Isaac pushed his hand through his hair. "Coffee?"

"No thank you. I just finished a latte from Jump Start. I don't want to leave here vibrating."

"Mind following me to the kitchen?" Isaac asked. "I've only had one cup, and I didn't sleep well last night."

"Stress?" Hannah guessed as she trailed after him.

"I'm sure you didn't come over to listen to my complaining. You said you had a question?"

Somewhere upstairs, a ladder scraped across the hardwood floor. "I'm wondering if there were others like Violet."

"Violet." Isaac said the name reflectively, as if he were trying to place it. "Violet."

"The bride with the canceled wedding?" Hannah prompted, a little surprised he needed to be reminded. The damaged relationship weighed so heavily on Amelia that she would have understood immediately what Hannah was asking. "Were there any others you had to cancel when the opening date moved? Are there other people who might be angry at you and Amelia?"

Isaac frowned as he thought. "That was our only wedding. And we hadn't taken many reservations yet because we haven't done much by way of advertising."

"Really?"

Hannah's surprise must have been evident in her tone, because Isaac added, "Aunt Amelia wanted to, but I cautioned against it. Better to get our feet under us before we start making much of a push for customers, you know? It turned out to be the best choice too, given all the renovation delays."

"Though you also might not get a chance to get your feet under you if you don't advertise." After the words were out of her mouth, Hannah realized it was none of her business. "Sorry, I shouldn't overstep."

Isaac shrugged, seeming indifferent. "I don't really know what the chances are of this place making it anyway. Not with an established place like Blackberry Inn already in town. Can Blackberry Valley even support two inns?"

For a moment, Hannah could only blink at him. Then she said, "If you don't think the bed and breakfast is a good idea, why are you here?"

She thought the question might make Isaac defensive, but he didn't visibly react. He sipped his coffee, the steam briefly veiling his face. "I told you already that Aunt Amelia needed help, and I needed a job. I thought it was a good idea at the time, but now…"

Hannah waited, but after a few seconds, Isaac merely shrugged. She waited longer, but all he did was take another sip of his coffee. For someone who said he had a lot to do, he didn't seem to be in a rush to go do it.

"After everything that's happened, you don't think it's a good idea anymore?" she supplied. "Having to change the opening date, the water leak, the theft."

"Yeah." Isaac's cup clinked as he set it down and leaned against the counter. "There's just so many signs that say this isn't going to work. It worries me that Aunt Amelia keeps pushing."

If opening the Hot Spot had been this challenging, would Hannah have pressed on? She hoped she would have. Maybe not with the same level of optimism as Amelia, but surely she wouldn't have given up easily.

"It's her dream," Hannah said. "Dreams are worth fighting for."

Isaac's stoic expression softened into a smile. "Yes. You're right. I have dreams I'm fighting for too, so I guess it makes sense." He straightened, shoulders squared, jaw set. "I'd better stop worrying about my aunt and get to work."

Hannah nodded, though she wasn't sure she'd be able to stop worrying about Amelia. "I'll get out of your way then."

"My aunt has always been good at taking care of herself," Isaac said as he followed her to the front door. "She'll probably be home by dinner and laughing that we thought anything might be wrong."

Hannah had to force herself to smile. "I really hope you're right."

"I'll let you know if I hear anything." Isaac closed the door behind her.

Hannah hesitated before leaving the cover of the front porch. The drizzle had turned to sleet, and the tiny pellets of ice clinked against the gutters and the vehicles parked in the circular drive. She dashed for her car and started the ignition, deeply thankful for the invention of seat warmers. Her windshield wipers did well with the wintry mix, but she knew it was only a matter of time before they became too frozen to be effective. Road conditions would be dangerous before long.

Wherever Amelia was, Hannah prayed she was safe and sheltered from the coming storm.

Chapter Sixteen

"I feel like we're preparing to open the restaurant for nobody," Elaine said as she unlocked the front door that afternoon.

Hannah's gaze drifted across the empty parking lot outside the Hot Spot. It had been a long time since she'd seen a car drive by. Precipitation was light once more, and the roads were still wet rather than icy or slushy, but the temperature was steadily dropping, promising worse conditions on the way.

"You're not wrong," she murmured.

Elaine's cheeks puffed as she blew out a long breath. She fidgeted with a dangly earring. "I hate when we're slow."

"It's definitely not my favorite." Hannah found herself fussing with the buttons on her cardigan. Much like Elaine, she wasn't good at being idle. "Dylan called not too long ago. He isn't coming in."

"That's good to hear. I can't imagine ice improves Dylan's coordination."

"No." Hannah chuckled. "I wouldn't think so. Do you want to head home? You live a little ways out of town, so I understand if you'd like to beat the weather. I could cover for—"

Elaine shook her head. "I'm fine, thanks. I'll stay for now." She frowned at the door then out the window at the empty parking spots. "I think I'll wipe down the menus. I know we keep them clean, but I need something to do."

"Sounds good," Hannah said. "I'll hang out here."

Despite Elaine's thorough cleaning of each menu, she was still back at the hostess stand before anybody came in for a table. Thirty slow minutes ticked away before the arrival of three elderly women who shared a house within walking distance.

"Congratulations, ladies," Hannah said as Elaine showed them to a table. "You beat the rush."

One frowned at Hannah, not seeming to understand that it was a joke, but one smiled and the third laughed. Upon hearing the arrival of customers, Raquel's face took on the expression of a child being allowed to open a Christmas present early, and she hurried to the table to take their drink order. Hannah squelched her desire to go over and chat with the women. Most people did not come to a restaurant hoping to make small talk with the staff.

Hannah tried to keep herself busy, but there wasn't much for her to do since Jacob, Raquel, and Elaine were also trying to stay busy. Jacob typically restrained himself from adding too much flair to his plates these days, but each entrée went out with so much flourish that Hannah was tempted to tell him to tone it down.

The idleness of the near-empty restaurant made it harder and harder for Hannah to resist texting Isaac and asking—again—if he'd heard anything from Amelia. She opened her messages and reread his response from when she'd asked in the late afternoon.

NOTHING YET. I'M SURE SHE'S FINE.

Hannah knew that Isaac was worried too. He was trying to put on a brave face and not make her worry even more, but she still didn't find his response satisfactory. She drummed her fingers on the counter and wished she knew Jason Perez well enough to ask if she could see the text Amelia had sent him. Hannah wanted to see the words for herself, as if by doing so she could discern if Amelia had truly been the sender or not.

But of course Amelia was the one who sent the text. As hard as it was to imagine her leaving for a couple of days right before her big opening and being "unreachable," it was even harder to imagine somebody abducting her. Who would do that? Nobody, that was who.

Yes, somebody had stolen from Amelia. And yes, either that same person or someone else had likely caused water damage at the bed and breakfast. While those attacks were personal and terrible, they didn't involve doing harm to Amelia herself. Hannah didn't fully trust Adam or Violet or Sabrina to have Amelia's best interest at heart, but she also couldn't imagine any of them sinking so low as to kidnap a woman in her midsixties. That made no sense.

The evening dragged on. Hannah gave up on occupying herself with restaurant tasks and called her dad to make sure that he and Uncle Gordon were at home and had no plans of going anywhere.

"Yep, we're home," her dad confirmed. "I've even got Zeus in his sweater. He's not so keen on it, but it keeps him warm when he goes outside. I'll send you a picture."

Hannah grinned. Zeus wasn't a spoiled dog, exactly, but he was a beloved dog. "I'm looking forward to it. Have you talked to Drew or Allison? Do you know if they're at home?"

"Yes, honey. I talked to Drew this afternoon. We're all home and safe. Quit your worrying."

Still, Hannah texted Drew after hanging up with her father. There were some sisterly instincts that didn't go away simply because her brother was married and had three children of his own.

When the clock finally struck seven o'clock and only one table was occupied, Hannah encouraged Elaine and Raquel to leave before the streets got any worse. She was tempted to send Jacob home as well, but aside from her, he lived the closest. Hannah didn't think it would go well if she attempted to be hostess, waitress, and cook for the boisterous table.

She watched Elaine's and Raquel's cars crawl away from the Hot Spot and prayed fervently for their safety. She thought it might be time to lock the doors and call it a night after the current diners cleared out.

The ringing phone jarred Hannah loose from her thoughts.

"The Hot Spot," she answered. "How can I help you?"

"Hi." The voice on the other end of the line was young and female, perhaps someone in her late teens or early twenties. "This probably sounds odd, but I'm wondering if my dad is there right now. I just got home and he's not here, but he often eats dinner at your restaurant. So I just thought I'd call and check."

Hannah's gaze swept across the restaurant. The lone occupied table was one of mixed generations celebrating a milestone birthday. They all wore party hats, and the adults seemed more enthusiastic about the whimsical touch than any of the children.

"It's possible. What's your father's name?"

"Adam Bristow," the girl said. "This is his daughter, Megan. He didn't expect me until tomorrow, but with the weather, I decided to hurry home today after my last final."

"Sorry, Megan. I haven't seen Adam tonight. I assume you've tried calling him?"

"Yeah." Megan's voice was tight with worry. "Calls go straight to voicemail, like his phone is off or out of range or something. But what's weirder is that I texted him this morning when I decided to come home early, and he never replied. I didn't think much about it at the time because Dad can be pretty iffy about responding to texts, but now that I'm here and he's not..." She blew out a long breath. "I'm sorry, I don't mean to ramble at you."

"No, you're fine, Megan. I completely understand why you're worried. I wish I had more information, but the last time I saw your dad was a couple of nights ago when he was in here for a takeout order."

"Okay." Megan sounded deflated. "Before I left for college, I tried to talk him into putting one of those apps on his phone so I could always see where he was. He said that was the dumbest thing he'd ever heard of. That when he was a kid, people didn't even have cell phones."

Hannah detected the rising panic in Megan's voice. "He's probably at a jobsite or something. He was telling me recently about a big remodel in Cave City."

"You're right. I'm sure I don't need to worry." But Megan's voice made it clear that she would absolutely worry until she was able to contact her dad, and Hannah didn't blame her.

"What about your grandmother?" Hannah asked, thinking of Adam sitting across from his sour-faced mother. "Have you tried calling her?"

"Yes, right before I called you. She hasn't talked to him either, but she said he eats here two or three times a week, so I should call you and ask. Said you're the best restaurant in town."

"Did she?" Hannah couldn't resist a grin, remembering that Adam's mother had eaten every bite of her cauliflower steak. "I'm glad to hear that. If your dad comes in, I'll call you right away. We're slow because of the weather, so I'll definitely notice if he arrives. Is the number you're calling from the best one for reaching you?"

"Yeah, this is my cell."

"Okay. My name is Hannah. If you hear from him, do you mind calling back and letting me know?"

"Sure," Megan said. "Thanks, Hannah."

Hannah disconnected the call and made a note on a pad of paper with Megan's phone number.

Jacob leaned out of the kitchen, a hopeful expression on his face. "New order?"

Hannah gave him a sympathetic smile. "Afraid not. That was Megan Bristow looking for her dad. You haven't seen Adam today, have you?"

"No, but that's not strange. Everybody's at home." He gestured to the mostly empty restaurant. "Except for these eight people."

"That's the thing though. Megan came home a day early from college, and he's not at home."

Just like Amelia wasn't at home.

Hannah's stomach clenched at the thought. Surely it was a coincidence. And it was also a coincidence that Megan couldn't reach her father by phone, the same as no one could reach Amelia by phone. The whole situation was one big coincidence.

Wasn't it?

Hannah awoke late the next morning, and the sight outside her window took her breath away. Blackberry Valley lay under a glaze of ice, glittering even in the weak sunlight. The fact that Christmas was only six days away made the whole scene feel that much more magical. Even if all this ice meant another slow day at the Hot Spot, the sight was so wonderous, Hannah didn't mind.

Before starting coffee, she reached for her phone to see if she had any updates from Isaac, or if—*please, Lord*—Amelia herself had called or texted her. But no. Drew had finally texted back his assurance that they were all okay, Lacy had sent a picture of Sprout with ice on her sweet little goat horns, and Liam had sent a brief text confirming that he was safe. All good texts to receive, but nothing from Amelia or Isaac.

Nothing.

Hannah bit her lip and reminded herself that Amelia was not *missing*. She had told Jason she was leaving town for "a day or two." Today was the beginning of day two. And she'd said she'd be unreachable, so all of this was what Amelia had told them to expect. While none of them knew where she was, that was different than her being missing.

Adam was a different story though. He really might be missing. While Hannah's coffee percolated, she went downstairs to check the messages at the Hot Spot. They'd closed early last night, so she was hoping a call had come in from Adam's daughter, but no. Hannah called Megan, but after several rings, the call went to voicemail.

Now what? Hannah drummed her fingers on the counter, but no brilliant insights arrived. Maybe the answer would become clear after coffee.

She took her time with breakfast, relishing sourdough toast and an omelet with goat cheese and chives. She sat in front of her window and looked out at the empty streets and glittering rooftops. More than anything, she longed to move to the couch with a cozy blanket and a good book, but there was too much to do to let herself fritter the morning away. For some items on her list, she'd have to wait for the roads to be safe again, but there were others she could take care of in the meantime.

She needed to take a bag of table linens to the cleaners, and she probably had linens to pick up as well. That was just a few doors down, so she might be able to walk there, assuming the sidewalks weren't sheets of ice. She should call her dad again and make sure he and Uncle Gordon were still doing okay. She could also figure out her contribution to Christmas dinner at Drew and Allison's house. Plus, a couple of invoices had arrived yesterday, and those needed to be paid.

Maybe by the time she was done with those things, the roads would be safe to drive on. She really needed to go pick up a sweater for Lacy's Christmas gift from that clothing boutique—one Lacy had admired when they were shopping together. Hannah had called when she was alone to place a hold on the sweater. Now she wished she had slipped back into the store while Lacy was preoccupied elsewhere. On the other hand, there were a couple of things she could only get at the market in Glasgow, so the trip would be useful in other ways too.

Hannah pulled on her boots and winter jacket then grabbed the bag of linens from downstairs. Outside, the clouds seemed a little thinner than they had been yesterday. She searched for signs that the sun was gaining strength but couldn't quite convince herself. When a car drove by, the roads appeared more slushy than icy. Hopefully, she could pick up Lacy's sweater sooner than expected.

Hannah assumed the cleaners would be as empty as the Hot Spot had been last night, so it surprised her when she approached the shop and saw through the front window that Katrina was assisting someone. Someone who was yelling at her.

"...completely ridiculous." The woman's voice came muffled through the glass. "I'll have to have this cleaned in Louisville, where they actually know what they're doing."

Hannah slowed her steps. She didn't want to eavesdrop, but she also didn't want to walk in during an argument.

The decision was made for her. The door burst open as the woman stormed outside. Hannah jumped at the sight of Sabrina, wearing a fierce expression that seemed a little comical when paired with her puffy down jacket and winter hat, both of which were bright pink.

"Oh." Sabrina blinked a few times at the sight of Hannah. A flush colored her cheeks, and she held a white wool coat to herself like armor. "Hi. How are you, Hannah?"

"Fine. How are you?"

"Same as usual. Trying to get a million things done, only now there's ice." Sabrina gestured to their surroundings. "I've had a slew of cancellations that I'm supposed to refund because the weather isn't their fault. Well, it isn't my fault either. And it isn't like this storm means I don't have to pay the bills, because I do. I'll see you later." With that, Sabrina stomped off down the sidewalk, slipping once but remaining upright.

"Bye, I guess," Hannah said to Sabrina's retreating figure.

When Hannah entered the cleaners, Katrina raised her head with fear on her face. The fear melted into a warm smile, but anxiety remained in her eyes. "Hello, Hannah. How are you this morning?"

"I'm doing better than Sabrina, I'd say. Are you okay? I couldn't help but overhear her yelling."

Katrina's smile was thin. "I don't like conflict. Especially with longtime customers. I like to make people happy."

Hannah infused her smile with empathy. "Not all customers can be made happy."

"True." Katrina began filling out the order form with Hannah's information. "Especially ones who expect me to work miracles. It's not my fault she got tar on her coat. She should be more careful."

"Tar?" Hannah echoed. "How on earth do you get tar on something in this day and age?"

"By going to Louisville," Katrina said with a chuckle. "Maybe it's not tar. I don't know. What do they use now when resurfacing roads? It's whatever that is."

Hannah remembered the black muck that had been on Isaac's SUV after he'd been to Louisville to get the commercial mixer. "I'm not sure what that is either."

"I've had a few come in this week with whatever it is on their clothes. The construction between here and Louisville has been good for business." Katrina chuckled, and then her face darkened. "Or maybe bad for business. It is very tough to get out completely. Most have understood, but others…"

Hannah smiled. "Others are Sabrina Hill?"

Katrina smiled back. "Exactly. She doesn't bring in many clothes, but she often refers hotel guests. Or if something gets particularly stained, she brings it here. I'm concerned about how this will affect my relationship with her."

"I'm sure she'll still recommend you, Katrina. She isn't going to tell people to drive to Cave City or Glasgow if they need something cleaned."

"True." Katrina's smile soured. "But there's little satisfaction in getting business because you're the only option. It's much more satisfying to feel as though you've earned the business."

"You do wonderful work, Katrina. Don't let Sabrina rattle you."

"Thank you."

Katrina picked up the bag of linens and disappeared into the back to find Hannah's clean items. Hannah mulled over Katrina's words. For a long time, Sabrina had been the only hotel option for those wanting to stay in Blackberry Valley. There were several chains close to the interstate, but nothing else in town limits. Katrina might chafe against the idea of receiving business by default of being the only dry cleaner in town, but did Sabrina feel the same about being the only inn?

If Sabrina was worried about how Sally's would affect Blackberry Inn's business, Hannah couldn't fault her for that.

There were other restaurants in town, but they weren't similar enough to one another to be much of a threat. They complemented one another. But how would Hannah feel if another farm-to-table place came into town? She'd probably get a little edgy too.

On the other hand, being stressed about competition didn't naturally lead to sabotaging pipes or stealing family heirlooms. Besides, the police had already questioned and cleared Sabrina. Hannah needed to stop searching for signs that Sabrina had it out for Amelia.

By the time Katrina brought out the bag of clean laundry, she seemed in much better spirits, gushing about how much she loved the butternut squash and parsnip soup currently on the menu at the Hot Spot. After some friendly chatter about favorite soups and a promise that her linens would be ready for pickup on Monday, Hannah carried her bag of clean laundry back to the restaurant and put everything away.

She checked messages on the restaurant phone once again, hoping for an update from Megan about Adam, but the only message was from Amos Bowers about a beef order. Should she call Megan again? Hannah had a hard time believing that Adam's absence could be connected to Amelia's decision to leave town, but the timing was strange.

On a whim, she called Isaac. His phone rang several times and then went to voicemail. She tried Amelia again. Hers went immediately to voicemail with the same message from yesterday—saying she was unavailable and if the call was in regards to Sally's, they should call the main number to speak to Isaac.

Hannah hadn't thought about it yesterday when she'd first heard the recorded message—probably because Amelia's departure had been such a shock—but now it struck her as odd. If Hannah was to leave town and was going to be unreachable, she would leave Elaine in charge. But she would also *tell* Elaine she was doing that. Wouldn't Amelia have done the same and told Isaac?

There were dangers in trying to puzzle out somebody else's decisions through the filter of what she would do. She and Amelia were different people, so Hannah couldn't assume that Amelia would think about things the way she did.

Still, she couldn't help thinking it was odd that Amelia had told Jason she was leaving, but not Isaac.

Chapter Seventeen

Hannah's Friday morning was peppered with text messages from Liam. As they'd discussed, her work responsibilities had slowed to a crawl due to the ice, while he could barely keep up with everything being thrown at him. Cars had slid off the road, roads hadn't yet been treated, and the power was out in more rural areas, which meant an uptick in generators and space-heater usage. All of that translated into more emergency calls than usual. And everything that had managed to melt during the day was expected to refreeze overnight.

So Hannah was surprised when an actual phone call came in from Liam. "Hi," she greeted him. "I can't believe you have time to call."

"I wanted to let you know that the roads are safe again. They won't be after sundown when the temperatures drop, but they are now."

"Okay, great." Hannah parked in a spot close to the shop she wanted in Glasgow, grinning. It was sweet of him to make sure she knew, even if the news was a bit late. "That's really helpful to know."

She popped her door open, which was apparently louder that she realized, because Liam said, "Wait, are you already in your car?"

"Yes?" The word curled into a question. "I needed to pick something up in Glasgow."

"You drove all the way to Glasgow?"

"I checked the road conditions before I left," Hannah said. "In case you're wondering, the highway between Blackberry Valley and here is wet but not slick."

"Did you really have to go the day after a winter storm?"

"Liam Berthold, I have survived this long making decisions about when and where I can drive without first receiving permission from the fire chief. You can trust me."

"I trust you. It's everybody else on the road I'm worried about."

Hannah laughed. It was the exact same thing her parents had said the first time they came to visit her in California and experienced Los Angeles's famous traffic. "I already have a father, thank you. But I *do* appreciate you calling and letting me know."

"Fine," Liam grumbled. "Will you at least text me when you get back into town so I know I can stop worrying?"

"Of course," Hannah said, smiling.

No, she didn't *need* Liam to make a fuss or to worry about her, but she had to admit that it was nice.

Hannah tucked her phone into her purse and headed inside the clothing boutique, which was more crowded than she expected and smelled like the sugar cookies that were being served near a Christmas tree. Despite having been there a few days before with Lacy, Hannah had a hard time not peeking at the new arrivals.

As she eyed a cream-colored sweater and debated if she should take the time to try it on, an oddly familiar voice said, "Can I help you find anything?"

Hannah turned toward the sales associate, and her eyes widened. Violet.

"Oh, Hannah." Violet's expression mirrored the surprise Hannah felt. "I didn't recognize you."

If she had, Hannah doubted Violet would have come over to check on her. She put on a polite smile. "How are you?"

"Good." Violet gestured at the crowd in the store. "Busy."

Hannah nodded. "I wouldn't have guessed it would be today. Hardly anybody was out in Blackberry Valley."

"I think you got it worse than we did," Violet said. "And we're only days away from Christmas, so not much will keep people out of the stores right now."

"That's why I'm here, actually. I'm picking up a gift. It should be on hold for me."

"It'll be in the back then. What's your last name?"

Considering how many highly emotional exchanges Hannah had either witnessed or experienced with Violet, it struck her as laughable that Violet didn't know something as basic as her last name. "Prentiss."

Violet nodded. "I'll go check."

Hannah walked away from the tempting sweater and loitered near the back door Violet had disappeared through. This was an unexpected opportunity to ask her more about Amelia. She could ask if she had heard from Amelia in the last twenty-four hours, though that seemed unlikely. Or she could ask more about the break-in. Hannah wished she had ideas for how to ask questions without setting Violet off. She'd yet to have a successful interaction with her.

Maybe she should try for an apologetic approach, though what would she be apologizing for? She certainly wasn't going to apologize for defending Amelia. Or for thinking that Violet might be involved in what had happened at Sally's, considering when Hannah had first encountered Violet, she was threatening Amelia.

Hannah continued to mull this over as she perused a display of necklaces. She didn't wear much jewelry, but she always liked browsing. Attached to one of the necklaces was an oblong pendant reminiscent of a rolling pin. Hannah cupped the pendant in her palm. She didn't think it was intended to be a rolling pin—the pendants in this row all varied slightly from one another—but that was what the shape made her think of. She could give the necklace to Amelia as a congratulations for the opening of Sally's.

"Sorry it took me so long," Violet said as she returned. "It's more cramped than usual back there, so it's harder to find things. That's pretty."

Hannah tilted the pendant so Violet could see it better. "Do you think it looks like a rolling pin, or is that just me?"

Violet cocked her head. "I can see it. Like a rolling pin in an impressionist painting."

Hannah chuckled, and it wasn't even forced. "Yes, exactly." She lifted the necklace off the rack. "I'll get this too. I think Amelia would like it."

Violet's smile stiffened, but all she said was, "Would you like me to wrap these for you?"

That would be more time to talk and one less thing Hannah needed to do, which made it worth the extra charge. "That would be lovely. Thank you."

Hannah trailed Violet to the table near the register where employees rang up and wrapped the gifts. After Hannah had paid for her purchases and picked out which paper she wanted, Violet surprised her by saying, "So, Sally's is finally going to open?"

Because Violet's back was to her, Hannah couldn't see her expression, but her tone was even.

"Yes, on Monday." Hannah hesitated. "Do you know that we're unsure where Amelia is right now?"

Violet whipped her head around to face Hannah, and Hannah was surprised by the emotion in the young woman's eyes. "What?"

Hannah swallowed. "Yeah. It's really strange. She told her contractor that she would be gone for a day or two and that she'd be unreachable. But she didn't tell anybody where she was going. Not even her nephew."

Violet stared at Hannah for so long that Hannah began to wonder if the woman had heard what she said.

"And you probably think I'm involved somehow," Violet finally said, her voice hoarse. "That's why you're here."

"No, it's not," Hannah said. "Like I told you, I'm here to pick up a gift. I had no idea that you'd gotten a job here."

Violet held her gaze for another moment and then looked away. "You might find this hard to believe, but I can't tell you how often I've regretted my words to Amelia that day at the B&B." She wasn't wrapping anymore, just staring at the boxes. "I've always had a short temper. My mom used to tell me that if I didn't learn how to control it, someday it was going to get me in trouble. And here I am."

This Violet seemed different than the Violet Hannah had run into other times. She wasn't quite sure what to make of it. Was this an act? Or had Violet really come to see that she'd made a mistake and truly regretted her actions?

Hannah took a tentative step closer. "Violet, are you in trouble?"

Violet huffed a humorless laugh. "In a way. I didn't do anything to hurt Amelia, and that's the truth. Well, I *did* write a mean-spirited social media post, but I took it down a few days later. And I *did* scream at her when she didn't deserve it. I *did* blame her for my canceled wedding, even though that was my own fault. And I *did* threaten her, which has meant that anytime something has gone wrong at Sally's, people have thought I was involved."

Violet met Hannah's gaze, and in that moment, she looked very young. She was probably only twenty-five or so. Hannah had said and done a lot of things at that age without thinking them through. She *still* made that mistake, though thankfully not as often.

"That's true," Hannah said quietly. "You did all those things."

"My life has really strayed from my intended course. I don't really know what happened."

Hannah heard the note of sorrow in Violet's voice. Yes, this was genuine remorse. She wanted to wrap an arm around the young woman's shoulders, but she wasn't sure how that would be received. "That happens to everybody sometimes."

Violet's voice was tight, as if she was trying not to cry. "I was valedictorian in high school, and now I have police showing up at my apartment because they think I might have stolen from an old woman. And I can't blame them for the suspicion, because I *yelled* at and *threatened* that woman. How did I become this person?"

Hannah didn't have answers for that. "Obviously, I don't know you very well, but I do know that you have a fire inside you that suggests you're capable of redirecting your life. Not to say it wouldn't be hard, but I think you can do it." Hannah recalled the conversation she'd intruded upon in Blackberry Market. "You and Lacy have a mantra from your spin class, right? Something your teacher used to say?"

Violet's mouth quirked. "'We can do hard things.'"

"Do you believe that?"

Violet shrugged. "I guess so."

"I believe you can do hard things. And I think going through these seasons makes us better people in the long run. Trials give us opportunities to persevere, and when we persevere, our character grows. I'm not saying it's easy or pleasant, but I think getting your life back on course boils down to making the next right decision."

Violet frowned. "What do you mean?"

"I mean when we wander away from a good path, we tend to think that it'll be a long walk back, but I don't believe that's true. I think the good path, the right path, is always right there beside you. There could still be consequences from when you were on a bad path, but you can always choose to get back on the good path."

Violet nodded slowly. "I think I know what you mean. The consequences from letting my temper get the best of me might linger for a while, but that doesn't mean I have to keep creating new situations like that."

"That's exactly what I'm saying."

Violet resumed wrapping the box. "Remember how I was searching for a new job that day at the coffeehouse? I have a second interview for a job at home. As a speech pathologist at an elementary school. That's what I went to school for."

"That's great," Hannah said.

"I never thought I'd want to return, but I really miss it."

Hannah nodded. "I moved back to Blackberry Valley not long ago, and I'm so glad I did. But it was important for me to move away too. Sometimes that's how you figure out what matters."

Violet smoothed the edge of the wrapping paper. "Do you think it's too late for me to apologize to Amelia?"

"It's never too late to apologize. I think that would mean a lot to her," Hannah said, though the mention of Amelia caused worry to slide through her again.

Violet bit her lip. "Okay. I'll think about what I want to say and give her a call. Though it sounds like I don't need to rush, since she's not answering her phone right now."

"She's not."

Violet gazed at Hannah. "Do you think something bad happened to her?"

"I don't know what to think," Hannah admitted on an exhale. "She told her contractor she would be gone a day or two, so it isn't as if she vanished into thin air. But when I was renovating the Hot Spot, I never would have left right before the opening. There was far too much to do."

"She has her son though, right?" Violet secured a piece of tape on the present. "Or, rather, her nephew? Maybe she passed all those things on to him to do."

"Yeah. Although he doesn't know where she is either. Or when she's coming back. He's as in the dark as we are."

Violet frowned. "That's strange."

"Isn't it?" Hannah asked. "I'm just hoping she comes home soon, because I'm worried."

"Amelia is very tough." Violet fixed a bow on the front of the second gift and handed them both to Hannah. "I think she'll be okay."

"I think you're right," Hannah said.

But worry still simmered as she drove back to Blackberry Valley.

"Do you think we'll still have the breakfast at Sally's on Monday?" Lacy asked.

Hannah had stopped by the Minyards' house on her way into town and found Lacy checking the heaters in the hen coop to make sure her beloved chickens didn't get too cold.

Hannah tugged her hat lower over her ears. "I assume so, but I'm really not sure."

Her weather app said it was forty degrees outside, but the clouds and the wind made it feel colder. She had no trouble believing Liam was right that the roads would refreeze after sundown. It was likely going to be another slow night at the Hot Spot. Hannah tried not to worry too much about the financial ramifications of two very slow nights in one week, especially with today being Friday, traditionally one of her two busiest nights.

"Surely Amelia will be back by then." Lacy frowned at the extension cord and tried again to get it to lie flat on the ground. "She's always said that Isaac is great in the kitchen, but of course only Amelia knows the recipes for the sweets, and that's what everybody is going to come there for."

"Somebody else knows too," Hannah reminded her. "Whoever broke into the safe."

"My money *was* on Violet, but after what you told me about your talk with her this morning, I've changed my mind." Lacy stood, finally seeming satisfied with how the cord lay. "Why did you have to go back to that store, anyway?"

"Just some last-minute shopping." Hannah felt especially glad that she'd bought the present for Amelia. "I found a nice necklace for Amelia while I was there."

"How sweet. So if Violet didn't do it, then I guess Adam is our most likely suspect now. I wonder if his daughter has found him yet."

"I'm not sure. She doesn't have my cell phone number. She'll call the Hot Spot if she hears from him, so I'll have to check messages when I get back." Hannah looked at the time. "I should go soon, actually."

"Do you have time to see the kids before you go?" Lacy asked with a wink.

Hannah grinned. "An aunt always has time for that."

"I'm keeping them in the barn overnight, with this weather," Lacy said as they set off that direction. A gust of wind hurled itself across the valley. "Maybe Adam took the money and the jewelry and went to Mexico. That sounds pretty good right about now."

Hannah shivered. "It sure does. What I still can't decide is whether the recipes were the point of the robbery, or if the cash and the jewelry were. They're both valuable, in different ways."

The wind gust grew stronger, and Lacy grimaced. "Maybe *Amelia* emptied out the safe and *she's* in Mexico."

Hannah couldn't help laughing at that. "If we were talking about Sabrina, I might believe you. She doesn't seem to like living here."

Lacy pulled the barn door open and ushered Hannah inside. "Do you remember meeting her general manager, Chrissy? She told me she thinks Sabrina is trying to sell the inn to one of those companies that buys small, local places."

Hannah made a face. "They have those for hotels? We have them in the restaurant business, but I didn't know it happens with hotels too."

"Yep. Chrissy thinks that's Sabrina's dream—to sell the place and move somewhere glamorous."

Hannah folded her arms over her chest. "Wonder what her parents would think of that. And why would she take over the inn for them if she didn't want to live here in the first place?"

Lacy shrugged. "Family business? She needed a job? Maybe she didn't realize how much actual work it would be? Or maybe there's been conflict because Sabrina wanted to remodel and her parents didn't want her to?"

"True." Hannah nodded. "Maybe she'd prefer a place that's entirely her own."

As usual, the barn smelled of hay and animals. Hannah's eyes took a few seconds to adjust to the comparative darkness, and when they did, she spotted her favorite new additions at Bluegrass Hollow Farm, the young goats Flower, Niblet, and Sprout. She tried not to let on that Sprout was her absolute favorite—aunts weren't supposed to have favorites—but sometimes it was tough. Like now when the goat stuck her sweet, cinnamon-colored head through the fence, as if to greet Hannah.

"I would take you home with me," Hannah murmured as she rubbed the goat's ears, "except you would eat everything in my apartment."

"And then she'd start in on the Hot Spot," Lacy joked.

Flower and Niblet sauntered over, probably thinking Lacy had brought them food. Hannah affectionately rubbed their ears as well before saying, "I wish I could stay, but I better get to the restaurant."

"I hope it's busier tonight."

"Me too, although I think it's unlikely, with the weather. Or maybe people will feel so stir-crazy from being stuck inside that they'll come out in droves."

"I'll ask Neil to pick something up for us when he closes for the evening." Lacy winked at Hannah. "That way you'll have at least one customer."

Hannah chuckled. "I'm sure Jacob will appreciate it. Whenever we're slow, he starts dreaming up new menu items and I have to rein him back in. Last night he kept trying to talk to me about cheesecake."

"Cheesecake?" Lacy echoed. "What's wrong with cheesecake?"

Hannah made her way to the barn door. "His idea is that we should be selling whole ones that people can take with them."

"Well, I like cheesecake," Lacy said with a shrug. "I vote yes."

"I love cheesecake, but if I approved every direction that man wanted to take the Hot Spot, I can't even imagine what a confusing mess our menu would be. People wouldn't know if they should come to us for a ten-dollar sandwich, a seventy-dollar dry-aged steak, or an entire cheesecake."

Lacy laughed. "I say why choose? I'm sure you know what you're talking about, but it all sounds good to me."

"I'm all for mixing things up. That's part of why I love the idea of a farm-to-table place, since it necessitates an ever-changing menu. But if you don't specialize, if you don't know what your restaurant is at its heart, you could fail big-time. At least I convinced Amelia to narrow down her menu and rotate things out seasonally. She was going to run herself into bankruptcy the way she had it before."

"Probably encouraged on by Isaac," Lacy said. "He doesn't strike me as the type to cut costs. Neil said when he and Amelia came to Legend and Key to ask about some maps of the area as well as books for each of the rooms, Isaac was more than happy to spend Amelia's money. As much as Neil appreciates the business, he didn't like that."

"Of course he didn't, because Neil is a decent man."

"He is, isn't he?" Lacy said with a wistful sigh. "I do love him."

Hannah grinned, but then a thought occurred to her that made the grin slide off her face. "What if it's Isaac?"

Lacy sobered. "What do you mean?"

"The water leak, the robbery, and..." Hannah frowned as she thought of Amelia's mysterious absence. She couldn't make any sense of how Isaac would be involved with *that*. He'd clearly been concerned when he'd called.

"He's the one who *found* the water leak," Lacy pointed out.

"That's right."

"And he was in Louisville when the robbery happened. Or on his way back from Louisville. Remember?"

"Okay, yeah. That's true." Hannah shook her head. "Never mind. My blood sugar must be low or something."

"Are you safe to drive, or do you want a banana for the road?" Lacy asked with a teasing smile.

"I think I have a granola bar in my purse, but thank you."

"I hope tonight goes better than last night." Lacy pulled Hannah into a hug as they reached the driveway. "Let me know if you hear anything about Amelia. Or Adam."

"Will do."

With a wave, Hannah got in her car and drove to the Hot Spot, ready to face either the boredom or the busyness that the night would bring.

Chapter Eighteen

Hannah frowned out at the dining room. It was six thirty on a Friday night, and only half the tables were full. She should be grateful that even that many were occupied, considering the roads and sidewalks were slick, but she didn't look forward to reconciling her business accounts at the end of the month and seeing lower numbers.

"The Lord will provide," she murmured to herself as she continued to fuss with the ice maker. "He always does."

Hannah wouldn't go so far as to say she was skilled at fixing things around the restaurant, but she'd learned a while back that there were certain things worth knowing how to repair herself rather than having to wait around for a repairman. The ice maker, however, was pushing the limits of her knowledge. And the ice outside was cutting into her profits.

"Need some help with that?"

"Thank you, I'm—" Hannah turned away from the ice maker—and gaped at the man on the other side of the counter. "Adam!" She hopped down from the step stool. "I talked to Megan last night, and I've tried calling her a few times today. I've been really worried."

Adam's face reddened. "Oh, goodness. Sorry about that, Hannah."

"What happened to you? Megan sounded so concerned when I talked to her."

Adam hung his head with a sheepish expression. "Yeah, I was in Cave City and stayed later than I should have, given what the roads were like. On the way home, I got going faster than was safe for the conditions, and my truck spun out. I was fine, and there was nobody around me, but even still, it scared me. I could've been in a ditch. Could've hit another car. After that, I'm not sure the speedometer went past ten miles an hour the rest of the way home. Sure was a good surprise to get there and find my girl waiting for me."

"I'm relieved it was nothing more than that," Hannah said. "Were you there for a job?"

"A job?" Adam blinked at her as if it was a foreign word.

"Yeah, is that why you were in Cave City?"

"Oh." Adam ducked his head again, his blush deepening.

"It's none of my business," Hannah rushed to say. "I thought you said you had a big job in Cave City, that's all. Anyway, I called Megan a few times today, but I only got her voicemail."

"The reception isn't great at my place. Probably why."

Was it Hannah's imagination that Adam was avoiding eye contact with her? Because somehow the reception had been good enough that Megan had managed to call the night before. Hannah was relieved to see that Adam was okay, but his behavior seemed a little dodgy.

"I'm glad you made it home safely, and I'm sure Megan was too," Hannah said. "I'm ready for this ice to go away."

"It's not that bad out there tonight." Adam cast his gaze outside, where the precipitation made the streets so shiny, Hannah could see the reflection of the streetlights. "Wet, mostly."

"Okay, good," Hannah said. "Are you picking up an order?"

"I am."

"Let me see if it's ready."

Hannah didn't find it on the shelf where completed takeout orders were placed, so she headed into the kitchen. Jacob was braising pork chops at the range, and Dylan stood at the counter, loading his tray with finished entrées. On the computer, Hannah pulled up the open takeout orders. She didn't see Adam's name on the list, which concerned her until she noticed an open order for "Megan."

"Hey, Jacob, how close are you to finishing the order with the winter cobb salad and Five Alarm burger?"

"For Megan?" Jacob asked, looking at his own list of open orders.

"Yeah."

"Five minutes, unless you can do the finishing work."

"Okay, I've got it," Hannah said, walking over to the partially completed order.

"That reminds me, Hannah." Dylan lifted the tray, which wobbled, causing a swoop of dread in Hannah's chest before he steadied it. "A call came in for you earlier from a girl named Megan. Not about a takeout order though. She said to tell you that her dad's okay, that he got home late last night."

Hannah sighed. That would have been nice to know earlier. "Thank you, Dylan."

She resisted the urge to call after him "Be careful!" as he carried his tray precariously through the door into the dining room.

Once again, Hannah sent the staff home early, at nine this time, and set about finishing what little work there was to be done. The final guests of the night had departed shortly after eight, and the Hot Spot staff had been tidying up and prepping for the next day as much as they could while also keeping the kitchen open in case someone else came in. Nobody had.

After waving goodbye to everyone, Hannah puttered around, wiping surfaces that were already clean and refilling salt and pepper shakers that were already adequately full. She knew she could shut off the lights and head up to her apartment for the night—maybe curl up with a book and herbal tea—but she was feeling melancholy in her spirit, and it made her reluctant to close out the day.

She poked about her thoughts, searching for the source of her blue mood. For one thing, having the restaurant open the last couple of evenings had been more expensive than if she'd just closed. That didn't feel good, but it happened sometimes. Its occurrence during the Christmas season, which was usually a time when tables were packed, hurt a bit more than it would if this had been a random Tuesday evening in February.

Maybe some of her melancholy was related to her mom. She always missed her more than usual this time of year, because her mom had worked hard to make Christmas magical. Up until now, Hannah had been preoccupied with the restaurant and everything happening at Sally's, and she hadn't paused much to think about how Christmas would feel if her mom were still alive.

And there was also the nagging concern for Amelia. Today was the end of day two, and Hannah still hadn't heard anything more about her. With all the weather they'd had, shouldn't Amelia have checked in with Isaac, if only to let him know she was okay? Though, really, she shouldn't have been gone at all. Not with Sally's on the brink of opening. Amelia had worked so hard to get to where she was, had persevered through so much. Why would she leave now?

Hannah snorted at the memory of Lacy's suggestion, that Amelia had emptied out her own safe and caught a flight to Mexico. Of course, Lacy hadn't been serious, but Hannah wouldn't blame Amelia if she'd gotten fed up with the whole situation and headed south to get away from it all. Amelia had too much character for that though. As Isaac had suggested, she was probably just in Louisville or someplace like it, getting the last of what they needed for Sally's.

But if that was all she was doing, why wouldn't she communicate that? And why would she be unreachable? Calling Isaac and asking for an update might annoy him, but Hannah could be okay with that.

Isaac answered with a polite, "Hello, Hannah."

"Hi, Isaac," Hannah said. "Any news about Amelia?"

"No, I haven't heard anything from her."

Hannah groaned. "That's so strange."

"I know." Isaac sounded weary.

She bit into her lower lip and cast a glance outside. "What if she's hurt? What if her car ran off the road?"

"Believe me, every what-if scenario has been running through my head too. But I don't know what else to do. She's not technically missing, because of the text she sent to Jason. Even so, the police say they're keeping an eye out for her car. I'm out of ideas, other than giving the situation more time."

Isaac sounded stressed, and Hannah discovered that she was scrubbing at a scratch on the countertop. She stopped and made herself take a deep breath. "I understand what you're saying, but I really don't like it. Especially with the opening on Monday."

Isaac snorted. "You and me both. If she's not back by tomorrow, I'll have to start canceling reservations and—"

"No!" Hannah blurted. "Amelia would be devastated."

"I get that." Isaac sounded less polite now. "But I didn't sign on to run this place by myself. I might be able to manage the breakfast part, though even when I had my food truck, I always had help. But the afternoon coffee hour, with the baked goods and all that—that's beyond me." He paused then said, "Well, not the coffee. I can do that."

Hannah's thoughts raced. She couldn't let Isaac delay the opening. "What if I pitched in? The Hot Spot is closed on Mondays, so I could help with breakfast and bake some things for the guests' coffee hour. They wouldn't be Sally's recipes, of course, but at least you wouldn't have to cancel reservations."

"I don't know," Isaac said. "That's nice of you, Hannah, but it seems like a lot to ask. And what about Amelia's thank-you brunch?"

"Do you know who she invited?"

"I do. She left a list of names and numbers on the desk in the office."

"Okay. If Amelia's not back by Sunday, you'll need to call those people and tell them the brunch has been postponed. It doesn't make any sense to have a thank-you brunch if Amelia isn't there to thank people."

"That's true," Isaac said. "I can do that. But are you sure you're okay to provide what we need for opening on Monday?"

"It's not a good long-term solution, of course, but if we're just talking about a couple of days, it'll be fine. My restaurant doesn't open until four on Tuesday, so I should still be able to handle breakfast and baked goods for you before I need to get back."

Not that Hannah had any idea how she would handle her other responsibilities if she was doing breakfast and coffee hour at Sally's on top of the Hot Spot, but she could swing a schedule like that for a couple of days.

"I'll think about it," Isaac said. "But if my aunt isn't back by Tuesday, we've got a lot more to worry about than breakfast and a coffee hour." In the background, a dog began barking. "Thanks for the offer. I need to go. Bye."

"Bye, Isaac," Hannah said, though the call had already been disconnected.

She tucked her phone into her pocket. Surely Amelia would be home sometime tomorrow, and Isaac wouldn't need to cancel reservations. Amelia had worked so hard to get to opening day, and Hannah couldn't believe she'd miss it.

Or rather, that she'd *decide* to miss it.

A soft knock at the door made Hannah yelp. She spun around to find Liam's handsome face grinning ruefully on the other side of the glass. With a hand over her pounding heart, she hurried across the dining room to unlock the door for him.

"Sorry. I didn't mean to scare you," he greeted her, sweeping into the restaurant and bringing a bite of cold air with him.

"It's fine. I was lost in thought." Hannah's heart continued to pound, but for a different reason. He looked tired, with shadows under his eyes and several days of stubble on his face, but knowing it was because he'd been taking care of their community was heartwarming.

Liam gazed at the empty dining room. "Another slow night?"

"Yeah. It was better than last night, at least. Between five and seven, business was okay, but I think people came earlier to avoid being on the roads when they refroze. Our last guests left just after eight, so I sent everyone else home at nine."

He grimaced. "Sorry to hear that."

Hannah shrugged, as if she hadn't spent a part of her night stressing about the financial ramifications of the storm. "How was your day?"

"Full." He raked his hand through his black hair, which flopped back onto his forehead. "Very full. I'm exhausted, but I saw the lights were still on and you were in here, so I couldn't resist stopping by."

Hannah smiled up at him. "I'm glad you did. Are you hungry? Do you want something to eat?"

She could tell from the face Liam made that he was hungry but that he also didn't want to ask her to go to any trouble for him.

"Do you like soup? Jacob put the extra in the fridge tonight, and I can heat some up in no time. There's butternut squash and parsnip, or chicken tortilla."

Liam searched her face. "Are you sure?"

"It's really no problem. And I'm hungry too. Which one do you want?"

"I'm not sure what parsnips are, so chicken tortilla."

Hannah grinned. "They're a root vegetable and look like white carrots. I like them, but I like most things. I'll be right back. Help yourself to something from the drinks station."

Hannah strode past the ice machine, satisfied to hear that it was humming like the day it had been delivered, and into the kitchen. There was a lightness in her heart now that Liam had arrived.

Lonely, she realized. Part of her melancholy had been because she was feeling lonely. Which was a little odd, considering that she had lived alone for years and was accustomed to doing things on her own. She'd been with people much of the day...but not with Liam. She'd been feeling lonely specifically for Liam. Hannah wasn't sure how she felt about that realization.

Within ten minutes, she'd heated up two bowls of soup and rescued a round of sourdough bread that was on its last day of freshness and had been set aside for making croutons.

Hannah returned to the dining room with a full tray and found Liam meandering around, examining the decor up close. That was a little funny because it wasn't as though there was anything in there he hadn't already seen before. Nearly everything belonged to his grandfather, Patrick, and was on loan.

He gave her a warm smile. Despite his obvious weariness, Hannah thought he'd never looked as handsome as he did right now, standing in the Hot Spot with the glow of the Christmas lights brightening his face, exhausted from several days of caring for their community.

Hannah set the tray on a table near the window, which provided a stunning view of Main Street in all its Christmas loveliness. "I brought out a small bowl of the butternut parsnip soup so you can find out if you like parsnips. Or at least if you like the soup. It won't hurt my feelings if you don't. Not every dish is for every person."

Liam chuckled. "I'm sure it'll be delicious. Everything that comes out of your kitchen is. This is especially impressive, considering I dropped by without warning. I didn't know what to get you to drink, so I just got you a glass of water. Do you want something else?"

"No, water's great. Thanks."

Hannah smoothed her hair behind her ears, noting how fluttery her heart felt. Despite being in a public place, standing in a lit window on Main Street, this felt like more privacy than they typically had.

"I saw the temperatures are going to warm up again tomorrow," she said as she took a seat. "That should be good for both of us."

"Yes." Liam rubbed the back of his neck as he sat down. "I'll get some sleep, and you'll get a busy restaurant again."

"Busy is my favorite kind of restaurant," Hannah said, though "empty with the exception of Liam" was pretty ideal too. Maybe it was her new favorite.

Liam said a blessing over their food then began sharing about his day. The cars that had gone off the road, the emergency calls they'd had to respond to, and men who were late to their shifts due to ice, meaning he couldn't take the break he'd anticipated.

"I'm glad the worst has passed," he said. "Even now, the roads are more slushy than icy. It's not supposed to get as cold tonight."

"What a relief." Hannah's soup bowl was empty because she'd mostly been listening.

Liam gestured to his cooling bowl. "Now I guess it's your turn to talk so I can eat."

Hannah smiled. "Work has been pretty slow, of course. Typically around this time on a Friday we're still stacking chairs and cleaning floors. But outside of work, I've been busy."

Hannah updated Liam on her surprising conversation with Violet at the boutique earlier in the day and then about Adam coming in to pick up a takeout order.

"Still nothing about Amelia's whereabouts though?" Liam asked.

Hannah shook her head. "Not a thing. It's strange, right?"

"Very."

"Maybe I'm reading something into it I shouldn't, but it bothers me that Adam was gone at the same time Amelia went off the grid. Also, he was pretty evasive when I talked to him."

"About Amelia?" Liam asked.

"No, I didn't mention Amelia to him. He said he was in Cave City last night, and I asked him if he was there for a job. His reaction made me think he wasn't, but he never said why he was there." Hannah took a sip of her water. "I backed off after that. It's none of my business, after all. And I don't think Adam would do something crazy like abduct Amelia. What would be the point of that?"

"I agree. He wouldn't gain anything from it." Liam's face creased with a frown. "I'm guessing you followed up with Isaac today."

"Right before you arrived, actually. He said he still hasn't heard anything. That if Amelia isn't back soon, he'll start canceling reservations."

Liam winced. "That wouldn't be good."

"Not at all. I offered to step in and help cover the kitchen so he doesn't have to do that. I mean, obviously I don't have Sally's recipes, but Isaac used to own a food truck. He isn't helpless in the kitchen. Between the two of us, I think we could handle the breakfasts for a couple of days."

"That's really kind of you, Hannah." The way Liam smiled at her made her feel like she'd won some sort of prize. "I hope Isaac realizes how generous it is of you to offer."

"Thank you," Hannah said, smiling.

"I wish I could see the text she allegedly sent to Jason," Liam said. "Or better yet, I wish the police could. Maybe I've been watching too many TV shows, but that's the part that worries me. A text can be sent by anybody, and I can't figure out why she would've told Jason where she was going rather than Isaac."

"Maybe she did text Isaac and it just didn't come through," Hannah mused. "That happened to me the other day. Lacy sent me a text in the morning, but I didn't get it until the afternoon. No idea why."

"It *can* happen, but it's pretty rare. How many times has that happened to you?"

"Just this once," Hannah admitted. "As far as I know, anyway."

"I don't like it," Liam said. "I'm going to start making some phone calls tomorrow. The whole thing is too weird."

The word "weird" turned into an unintentional yawn. The poor man must be on the verge of falling asleep right there at the table.

Hannah stood and gathered the dishes onto the tray. "I think it's time for you to go home and get some sleep, Chief."

"I'll help you clean up."

"No, don't worry about that. This won't take long," Hannah said. But Liam trailed her to the kitchen anyway.

After they'd loaded everything in the dishwasher, Hannah walked him to the door. Liam's hand rested on her arm for several wonderful seconds before he gave her a hug and said a soft, "Good night."

"Good night," she replied. Her heart felt lighter than it had in ages.

As Hannah turned off lights and locked up the Hot Spot, she decided that she wouldn't mind if more evenings ended in leisurely conversations with Liam Berthold.

Chapter Nineteen

When Hannah unlocked the Hot Spot the next afternoon, there were already people waiting on the sidewalk, as if the residents of Blackberry Valley wanted to make up for lost time. She greeted customers as they came inside and helped Elaine get the guests settled. As soon as Hannah seated a large group of elementary school teachers celebrating the end of the semester one day late, she hustled back to the kitchen to help Jacob.

"I haven't worked this fast in days." Jacob grinned at her as he lowered a basket of wings into the fryer and simultaneously flipped chicken on the grill. "Feels great."

Hannah's cheeks hurt from how big she was smiling. "Doesn't it?"

Not only was the afternoon warm enough that the ice had been vanquished, but the sun was out in full force. Pedestrians strolled along in light jackets rather than winter coats, and Elaine didn't shiver every time the door opened.

Hannah was shocked when she looked up and realized it was already seven o'clock. Time moved so much faster—and more enjoyably—when the restaurant was packed.

When Elaine stepped out for her break, Hannah took over at the hostess stand. Once again, Sabrina sat on a bench out front, but without Togo this time. Hannah checked the computer and saw that Sabrina was waiting on a takeout order.

When it was ready, Hannah carried it out to her with a smile.

Sabrina grinned up at her. "Thank you."

"No problem. How are you? You seemed stressed when I saw you last."

Sabrina's expression was blank for a few moments but then lit with recognition. "Oh, right. At the cleaners." She grimaced. "Sorry you had to see that. For what it's worth, I called Katrina back and apologized."

"Did you have many more cancellations?"

"Only one cancellation and then several delays. Otherwise, everything ran as smoothly as I could have hoped for." Sabrina peered at her. "Sounds like I better be prepared for additional guests with the troubles at Sally's. Have you heard that Amelia is—I don't know what the best word is to use here. Missing? Unaccounted for?"

"Yes." Hannah considered taking a seat but leaned against the wall instead. "I'm really worried about her."

"Yeah." Sabrina fussed with the buttons of her blazer. Her pantsuit was reminiscent of the ones Hannah had seen on high-level executives in LA. As sharp as it was, Hannah couldn't help thinking it was out of place in Blackberry Valley. "Frankly, it's not a good look for someone who's about to open a hotel. I mean, *I* can't just take off like that. I haven't been more than a mile away from the inn since the beginning of the month, when I went to Michigan to see my nephew. And even that was an enormous pain."

Hannah frowned. "And Louisville, right?"

Sabrina blinked rapidly. "What?"

"I had in my head that you went to Louisville too, but I don't know why." The reason came to Hannah in a flash. "Oh, because of something

Katrina said about the black residue on your jacket. She said it was from roadwork that's happening between here and Louisville."

Sabrina's cheeks turned pink. "No, I, um, don't know where that came from. I bet I rubbed against a guest's car or something like that. We have lots of guests who come through on that highway."

"That makes sense," Hannah said, keeping her tone light. "I agree it's odd about Amelia. She's worked so hard, I'm having trouble imagining why she would leave and be unreachable."

Sabrina gave a shake of her head. "She'll figure out one way or another that when you own a place, that kind of thing isn't an option. You're not going to get breaks when you're running a successful business." She gestured toward the Hot Spot. "I thought if anybody would know where Amelia is, it'd be you."

"I would've thought Isaac. He's family as well as her business partner."

"They had a big argument earlier this week." Sabrina flinched. "I mean, that's what I've heard. That might not be true."

Amelia and Isaac had argued? Neither of them had mentioned that to Hannah. That wasn't surprising with Isaac, who was hardly the type to share his worries and concerns with her, but she did feel a bit surprised that Amelia hadn't mentioned a big argument. Unless maybe the phrase "big argument" was an overstatement.

"What did they argue about?" Hannah asked.

"I don't know." Sabrina dropped her gaze. "I don't know Isaac, so this is what I've heard from others. It sounds like Amelia has unreasonable expectations for him."

Hannah had never been under that impression. "Who'd you hear that from?"

"I can't really remember, honestly. Just one of those things you hear in a suffocatingly small town." Sabrina laughed and looked at her watch. "Is it really seven fifteen? I need to get back to the inn. See you later, Hannah."

And with that, Sabrina sauntered down the sidewalk, her bag from the Hot Spot swinging from her elbow.

Once upon a time, Hannah had also found Blackberry Valley "suffocatingly small." When she moved to LA, she'd loved going to the movies or the library or the market and not running into her PE teacher or middle school crush. Being one of so many had felt like she finally had the breathing room to figure out who she really was apart from who she'd always been in Blackberry Valley.

What she'd eventually found was that Hannah Prentiss loved her home. She'd thought Los Angeles was a destination, but really it had been a cocoon. When she finally emerged, she flew home.

Sabrina's information about a big argument continued to churn through Hannah's thoughts. Finally, she told Jacob, "I'll be back in about thirty minutes," and headed outside.

Main Street was full of holiday hustle and bustle. The line for Santa Claus had dwindled now that the sun had set, but the sidewalks still held lots of families heading to and from stores or restaurants. Hannah smiled at those she knew as she hurried toward her car.

She had considered calling Isaac again, but after thinking about it for a while, she decided this conversation was best in person. She wanted to be able to see his face when she asked about the argument.

Would he deny that it had happened? Claim that everything was fine between him and his aunt and that Hannah was making something out of nothing? There was only one way to find out.

Hannah pulled into the circular drive at Sally's, which was surprisingly empty. There were no construction vans or trucks. There were no sounds from within, and no one came to the door when she knocked. She tried the doorknob, but it didn't turn. How strange. She couldn't remember a single time that she'd come over there and found the door locked.

She walked around back toward the old gardener's house, where Isaac lived. His SUV was there and had been washed recently, because it didn't even have the gray, salty crust around the wheel wells that Hannah's did from driving on roads that had been treated for ice.

Feeling a little awkward, Hannah knocked on the door. After a few seconds, she heard footsteps approaching. When Isaac opened the door, the savory scent of frying sausage filtered out. He wore casual clothes—black joggers and a sweatshirt—but something about the way they fit made Hannah think they were expensive.

If Isaac was surprised to see her, it didn't show on his face. "How are you, Hannah?" he asked, his voice a low, warm rumble.

"I'm okay, thank you. I'm wondering if you've heard anything from Amelia?"

"Not a thing." Isaac leaned against the doorframe and gazed up at the bulky structure of Sally's. "I'll have to start making calls tomorrow to cancel guests."

His eyes were bloodshot and puffy, implying that he hadn't been sleeping well. Maybe Hannah shouldn't push him about the argument after all.

"Are you fully booked on opening night?" Hannah asked.

"Not until the twenty-third, but then we're full until January sixth." He rubbed the back of his neck. "I'm not too worried about taking care of the four guests for the first few days, but when we start talking about double that?" He shook his head. "I don't know that I can do it beyond that. I know you offered to help, Hannah, but you have your own business to care for."

Hannah didn't have a college degree in hospitality, but she was sure that canceling on guests was a bad way to start a new bed and breakfast. "She's worked so hard. Surely she'll be back by then."

Something flashed in Isaac's eyes. "Who knows what my aunt is thinking at this point? I mean, she didn't even tell me she was leaving town."

"Were you on good terms when she left?" Hannah asked. "Or had you been arguing?"

His gaze slid to meet hers. "We were fine."

Hannah pursed her lips and decided to press the issue. "Are you sure? I heard that the two of you had an argument right before she left."

Isaac's gaze remained steady on Hannah. After a moment, the corners of his mouth quirked into a grim smile. "This town is too small. Yes, we did."

"Then why did you say you were on good terms when she left town?"

"No disrespect intended, Hannah, but that isn't any of your business."

Hannah felt her cheeks going warm because he was right. "That's true. It isn't."

Silence stretched between them. What should she say now? The polite thing to do would be to walk away. Well, being polite had gone out the window when she asked about the argument in the first place. But how much more impolite did she want to be?

"When I heard about the argument, it seemed odd that you hadn't mentioned it any of the times that we discussed Amelia's absence," Hannah said, keeping her voice as gentle as she could.

Isaac's cheeks flushed. "I didn't say anything about it, because I was embarrassed. With how nosy everybody is around here, I figured people would think I was somehow involved in Aunt Amelia's disappearance. Like I'd done something sinister."

Now it was Hannah's turn to feel embarrassed, because she knew she was being nosy. She'd known it before she drove over there but had decided that it was worth it if she could get answers about Amelia and what had happened right before she left. And Isaac was also right that if she'd known about their argument earlier, she probably would have suspected that he was somehow involved in her disappearance.

Isaac peered at her. "It was a normal family argument. Don't you argue with your parents? Your siblings? It doesn't mean you're on bad terms. It wasn't like we were yelling and screaming at each other. We simply disagreed. It certainly wasn't worth Aunt Amelia leaving town."

But what had they disagreed about? If Hannah asked, he would probably tell her again that it was none of her business. And, again, he wouldn't be wrong.

"So you don't think the dispute was why she left?"

Isaac stuck his hands in his pockets and shrugged. "The thought crossed my mind, but I don't think so. On the other hand, I also would have said that Aunt Amelia would never leave town this close to the opening, so what do I know?"

Anxiety churned in Hannah's stomach. She really wished Amelia would just send a simple text to let them know she was okay. Remembering what Liam had said about texts, though, she would prefer a call.

"But," Isaac continued, "I think our disagreement the night before is probably why she told Jason she was leaving town and not me. Even so, I don't think she took off because she wants me to take over Sally's when she retires and I told her I have no intention of doing that."

"That's what you argued about?"

Isaac nodded. "Things could change of course, but this place is Aunt Amelia's dream, not mine. For me, it's a job while I get on my feet and save up for a place of my own, ideally somewhere more metropolitan." He glanced at her. "No offense."

How funny that she was having this conversation with Isaac so shortly after Sabrina had used the phrase "suffocatingly small" to describe Blackberry Valley.

"Small-town life isn't for everybody. I get that."

"I mean, when a routine argument that you have with your aunt becomes town gossip, it doesn't make a compelling case for living here long term," he said.

Hannah offered a sympathetic smile. "If it makes you feel any better, I really haven't heard many people talking about it."

She didn't bother to say that it had only been one person, and Isaac apparently wasn't concerned enough to ask more questions.

Hannah's mind worked through what Isaac had said. She knew Amelia had brought him into Sally's partly to help him out of a tough financial spot but also because she hoped to keep the place in the family. Hannah had no trouble imagining that Amelia would have been upset to learn that Isaac wasn't really interested in that, but it also didn't seem like the kind of revelation that would have sent her over the edge and caused her to flee town right before her grand opening. Really, it didn't seem like a revelation at all.

"I feel terrible about upsetting my aunt, of course." Isaac absently scraped at flaking paint on the doorframe. "But I couldn't let her hang all her hopes on something that's never going to happen."

Hannah considered this. She had no doubts that Isaac might have been harsher than necessary in how he delivered this news to his aunt, but he was right. If he had no intention of taking over Sally's for her, it was a good and necessary conversation to have. Amelia needed to know the truth.

"That makes sense," Hannah said with a nod. The wind whipped her hair in front of her face, and she shivered. It was about time for her to be getting along. "Sorry to be one more nosy town person, but I just can't stop worrying about where she's gone. So when I heard that the two of you had argued…"

Isaac shrugged. "I get it. I imagine I would've done the same thing myself if I'd heard that *you* and Aunt Amelia had argued."

Hannah recalled the morning of the robbery, when Isaac had returned from Louisville and fixed a suspicious gaze on her. Yes, she had no doubt that he would have done that.

"I really am happy to help with breakfasts and coffee hours if you need it. I know your aunt says you're great in the kitchen, but if you want an extra set of hands, I don't mind."

"This is where it'd be nice if Aunt Amelia—or my grandmother—had been the type to share recipes. Instead, they keep all these secrets." Isaac shook his head and started to push the door closed. "Thanks, Hannah. I'll be in touch."

Hannah walked around to the front of the B&B, where her car was parked, her hands in her pockets. She took in the impressive structure of Sally's and thought of Isaac's suggestion that they should have called it "Secret Sally's."

She wondered if elementary school students still chanted the same rhyme that she and her friends had as kids: *Secrets, secrets are no fun. Secrets, secrets hurt someone.*

Hannah fervently hoped that the "someone" who got hurt in this situation wasn't Amelia.

Chapter Twenty

Hannah had never been very good at wrapping gifts. She frowned at the awkward mess of red and green paper sitting on her coffee table. Would her dad care? Probably not, but *she* did. As much as she adored the lumpy packages she received from her niece and nephews, she didn't want her own wrapped gifts to be mistaken for theirs.

With a sigh, she began undoing the wrapping paper. As she did so, her phone lit up with a name. For a moment, Hannah gaped at it. Then, in her efforts to answer hastily, she dropped her phone, and it bounced under the couch.

With a groan of frustration, Hannah retrieved the phone and answered the call. "Amelia?"

"Hello, Hannah—"

"Thank You, God," Hannah said on an exhale. She leaned back into the couch, feeling her whole body relax. "Are you okay?"

"Yes, Hannah, I'm fine."

"I'm so glad." Tears sprang to Hannah's eyes, and relief washed through her like a wave. Like a wonderful, relaxing wave. "I've been so worried about you. Actually, a lot of us have been."

"That was not my intention," Amelia said in a solemn voice. "I was so sorry when I returned home and heard how distressed everyone was. Isaac sure gave me an earful. Told me I can't act like I'm living in Nashville, where people don't notice if you take off without a word. I did this all the time when I lived there and no one seemed to care, so it never occurred to me that it might cause such a stir. I'm deeply sorry."

"I'm happy to forgive you," Hannah said, "if you'll indulge my curiosity and tell me what happened. Where have you been?"

Amelia chuckled self-consciously. "I feel terrible saying this since it sounds like I caused a lot of stress with my actions, but I've been at a lovely cabin in the woods. Everything with Sally's had become so stressful, so all-consuming, that I'd lost sight of what mattered most. Of *Who* mattered most. I kept feeling the tug of the Lord to take time away with Him, but I kept ignoring it. 'Don't you know how much I have to do, Lord?' I kept saying."

Oh, sweet Amelia. Hannah thought back to their conversation when she'd been doing laundry and how Amelia had said she was out of sorts because she wasn't getting the time with God that she needed.

"So after you made that comment about how Sally's opened in a few days, I looked at my calendar and saw how many reservations we have. I realized that if I didn't get away *now*, I wouldn't get away for a very long time."

The idea that Amelia had been reconnecting with God in a cabin in the woods made Hannah smile. And, if she was honest, it made her feel a little jealous too. It sounded like a lovely way to spend a few days, especially as Christmas approached.

"I love that, Amelia," Hannah said. "I don't love that you won't be able to get away for a long time, but I *do* love that you took the time now."

"I just wish I hadn't made everybody so concerned. I figured Jason was the only one who would even notice I was gone. Well, and Isaac too. But I was feeling irritated with him when I left town. As terrible as it sounds, I knew he would find out I told Jason and not him, and I thought he'd realize then how upset I was at him." Amelia sighed.

"You weren't thinking very clearly when you left," Hannah said. "I imagine you would make a different choice now."

"Yes, I would. Poor Isaac. It's not his fault that he'd rather open his own place in the city than be saddled with mine."

Despite Amelia's words of acceptance, Hannah could hear the sorrow in her tone. The longing for her nephew to want the dream that she had.

"No, it's not," Hannah said. "But I understand that his desires feel disappointing to you. What kind of place did he have in mind?"

"A coffeehouse," Amelia said. "Well, coffeehouse and bakery, I guess. He's mostly interested in the coffee part, but he knows a more robust menu and baked goods are a good idea. I'm lucky he's broke, or he wouldn't be here at all." She gave a tight laugh. "He talked me into a fancy espresso machine for our coffee hour, so he'll get plenty of practice. And he'll gain valuable experience at Sally's learning from all my mistakes."

"And your successes," Hannah reminded her. "You're teaching him a lot about persistence. You're teaching us *all* about persistence, really."

"One foot in front of the other," Amelia said. "Sometimes that's all you can do. I knew if I didn't take time away, I'd be dragging myself across the finish line. And the finish line in this case—getting Sally's open—is actually the starting line. Dragging myself across a starting line sounded like a terrible idea. But now I'm excited to welcome my first guests. Can you believe it all begins tomorrow?"

"Yes," Hannah said firmly. "Because it feels like you've been trying to open this place for an eternity."

Amelia chuckled. "That's true."

Hannah anchored the phone between her shoulder and ear and smoothed the wrapping paper over the box. "Have you had any updates from Jacky Holt about the missing items in your safe? Or have you not had a chance to talk to her yet?"

"I spoke to her a little bit ago. It doesn't sound like they've been able to find anything yet. Which is disappointing, of course, but it's not the end of the world."

Hannah taped the wrapping paper in place. "I had an interesting conversation with Adam while you were away. I still don't know why he might have stolen from you, but he was missing from his home the first day you were gone too."

"Really?" Amelia said. "How strange."

"Isn't it? His daughter came home from college and was surprised when he wasn't there. He hadn't responded to her texts all day, and he wasn't answering his phone. Apparently, he arrived home very late that night. It was the day the ice came in, so he claimed he was in Cave City and drove home really slowly."

"But you don't believe him?"

"I'm not entirely sure what I believe," Hannah said carefully. She gave up on trying to wrap the gift while talking on the phone. "I think parts of his story are true, but he was reluctant to tell me why he was in Cave City. At first, I thought it had to do with your disappearing."

"Sorry," Amelia said. "I promise I've learned my lesson. Next time I'll send a text."

Hannah smiled. "I appreciate that. I know now that he wasn't involved in your absence, but maybe he was in Cave City to sell the jewelry or something like that? Now that he's already been investigated, I mean. I don't know. Maybe it's nothing."

"Maybe," Amelia agreed. "Wouldn't it be nice if someone would walk into the Hot Spot wearing a new suit that costs exactly the amount that was stolen and holding a platter of Sally's rosemary lemon shortbread?"

"That would be so convenient." Hannah chuckled. "It would really save us a lot of time too."

"Though whoever took the recipe box wouldn't be able to do that, I suppose."

"Why not?" Hannah asked. "Didn't your mother keep her secret recipes in there?"

"She didn't keep her secret recipes *anywhere*." Amelia laughed heartily. "My mother was a real believer in that passage from Deuteronomy that talks about teaching your children as you go about your life. She had her secret recipes memorized, and she taught them to me when I baked with her in the kitchen. She said that was the only real way to pass them on—side by side."

The whole time, Hannah had assumed that Amelia was upset about losing the recipe box because it meant the family secrets were out, but apparently not.

"If the box didn't have your secret recipes in it, then why did you keep it in the safe in the first place?"

"Because it's still precious to me. Lots of Mom's recipes are in there, just not the special ones. And the safe is fireproof. I figured if the place caught fire—and the way things are going, that didn't seem unlikely—then the best place for my box was in the safe. If someone like Violet or Sabrina took the box hoping to get my secret recipes, they were mightily disappointed."

"Sabrina is still a maybe," Hannah said, "but I think I've ruled out Violet." She caught Amelia up on her conversation at the clothing boutique with Violet. "Maybe she was lying, but I don't think so. She truly seemed remorseful."

"It would be really lovely if she was," Amelia said.

"She said she was going to call you."

"I haven't checked all my messages yet. I guess I should. I missed a lot these last few days, didn't I?"

"Not nearly as much as you gained, it sounds like," Hannah said. "I think you made the best choice, although next time it would be good for our hearts if you let us know why you'll be unreachable."

"I promise," Amelia said solemnly. "Are you still coming to the brunch tomorrow?"

Hannah grinned. "I wouldn't miss it."

Chapter Twenty-One

Hannah was delighted when she pulled back her bedroom curtains on Monday morning and saw the sun shining for Amelia's opening day. She knew it was a little silly, but she wanted Blackberry Valley to look its best for the hotel guests and make a good first impression on the visitors.

She paired a deep red sweater with dark jeans and black ankle boots, hoping for a festive vibe without being too over the top. After taking extra effort to curl her hair, she checked the time. There was a new text from Liam. Okay if we meet at Sally's? Had to pick up prescription for Gramps and am just now leaving his place.

Hannah texted back that it was fine and then considered what to do next. It was too early to arrive at Amelia's. She took a look at her list of errands and was happy to note that she needed to pick up the Hot Spot's linens from the dry cleaner. Perfect. She could take care of that and then head to Sally's.

She wasn't ten steps out the door when she saw Sabrina out for a walk with Togo. Of course the dog immediately started barking, despite Sabrina tugging at the leash and yelling, "Quiet!" The irony made Hannah chuckle. The nice thing about all the barking was that she didn't feel obliged to stop and have a conversation. She offered Sabrina a friendly smile and kept walking.

When she stepped into the dry cleaner's, she found that Katrina's college-age daughter, Hazel, was at the front counter assisting a customer. Both women turned and looked at her with wide-eyed expressions. After a moment, Hannah recognized the customer—Megan Bristow, Adam's daughter. Though she'd never seen Megan in such a state, with puffy red eyes and hair tumbling out of a messy bun.

"Hello." Hannah put on a smile. "I'm sorry to interrupt."

"No, you're not." Megan shook her head and stepped to the side. "I was just giving poor Hazel an earful. Don't let me slow you down."

"You're Megan, right?" Hannah said. "I'm Hannah Prentiss."

Megan blinked at Hannah, clearly trying and failing to place her.

"I own the Hot Spot," Hannah added. "We spoke on the phone the other night."

"Oh yes." Megan loosed a slight laugh. "Yes, of course. Sorry, I'm not really myself today."

She wore a university sweatshirt and plaid flannel pants. Hannah knew that many young women Megan's age didn't think twice about leaving the house in what Hannah would consider to be pajamas, but the few times she had seen Megan, Megan had been put together, with her hair down and a youthful glow. Now she just looked sad and tired.

"I'm sorry to hear that," Hannah said.

"It's not that big a deal," Megan said, although she sounded more like she was trying to convince herself than Hannah. "I'm overreacting."

"You're not overreacting," Hazel said without looking up from the pile of order tickets she was leafing through. "Having an emotional response isn't an overreaction."

Megan glanced at Hannah. "You know how I couldn't find my dad on Thursday and I was super worried? I found out he was in Cave City on a date."

Hannah thought of Adam's reaction to her question at the restaurant, the blush of embarrassment. The hesitation to share where he'd been. "I see."

"My mom has been gone a long time." Megan shrugged and pulled at the neckline of her sweatshirt. "So I'm not sure why it's bothering me so much. It isn't as if I want him to be alone forever."

"It's new." Hazel found the ticket she'd been searching for. "And it's normal for new things to feel uncomfortable. Even good things, like new shoes."

Megan actually chuckled. "You're comparing my dad's relationship status to new shoes?"

"I am." Hazel faced Hannah and asked, "Are you here to pick up those linens?"

Hannah nodded.

"Okay, I'll be right back."

Hazel hurried away, leaving Hannah alone with Megan and the whir of the machines.

"I guess they've been seeing each other for a few weeks." Megan blew out a breath. "Dad didn't tell me because he knew it would upset me."

"He cares about you."

Megan nodded. "And I know he's been lonely since I left for college. I can only imagine what business has been like. I used to take care of details like his schedule and sending invoices. He's good at what he does, but he's awful at the administration side. I worried about leaving him, and sure enough, he overbooked himself right away and lost the job at that old house being turned into a bed and breakfast."

"You can't blame yourself for that, Megan," Hannah said. "It's important to leave home. And your dad wouldn't want you to stay for him. For what it's worth, I lost my mom to cancer a few years back, and sometimes it's hard for me not to overstep when it comes to trying to take care of my dad. Sometimes we have to trust that parents can take care of themselves."

Megan laughed. "I guess. How else will they learn if we don't let them make mistakes sometimes?"

Hazel brought out the bag of linens and smiled when she saw Megan's face. "Oh, good. You're smiling."

Hannah paid her bill, wished both young women a good day, and headed out into the crisp, sunny morning. She peeked at the time and saw she might be a few minutes late. Fashionably late, as her mother always called it. She dropped the clean laundry inside the Hot Spot, grabbed the necklace she'd purchased for Amelia, and got into her car.

She pulled out of her parking spot and headed toward Sally's. She finally had the explanation of why Adam had acted so dodgy regarding his whereabouts on Thursday. Not that Adam having a girlfriend proved his innocence with the leak or the robbery, but his involvement in either incident seemed more and more like a stretch.

As Hannah passed Blackberry Inn, she remembered what Lacy had said about Sabrina trying to find a buyer for the place. Maybe when Amelia turned down Sabrina's offer to take over Blackberry Inn, Sabrina had decided to sabotage Sally's before Amelia could open a competing business.

Nope. That didn't work. Sabrina would have been Hannah's number one suspect, but she had been out of town the entire weekend the water damage had occurred. But what about the safe? She'd been in town for that.

Hannah frowned. If Sabrina was trying to harm Amelia's business, why break into the safe? Was it for the recipes? But, again, what would she do with those? She couldn't very well use them here in Blackberry Valley.

Hannah was so lost in thought that she nearly missed the entrance for Sally's. The driveway was already full of vehicles, including the Minyards' truck and Liam's Jeep. Hannah parked and stepped out of the car.

Even from outside, Hannah caught the delicious scents of Amelia's kitchen. Frying bacon and sausage and something yeasty. Cinnamon rolls, perhaps? Hannah's stomach growled.

Inside smelled even better. If Amelia could capture this aroma in a bottle, she could have a nice side business as a candlemaker. Hannah would buy a candle that reminded her of a homemade breakfast wrapped in a hug and dipped in cinnamon sugar. Warm chatter rose from the dining room and filtered into the entryway, and Hannah felt tears prick her eyes. Amelia had done it. All these months of perseverance had brought her here, to her opening day.

"Thank You, Lord," she whispered. "What a blessing."

In the doorway of the dining room, Hannah scanned the mostly full tables. Morning sunlight cast a lemon-yellow glow over the room. She spotted Liam sitting at a table by the window with Jacky Holt and her twin brother, Alex. The seat beside him was empty.

Hannah found Lacy several tables over. She was beside her husband and across from Zane Forrest, who had helped Amelia source her coffee. Sheriff Colin Steele and his wife, Geraldine, shared a table with Pastor Bob and his wife, Lorelai.

Lacy saw Hannah and smiled, then made a point of looking at the empty seat beside Liam and raising her eyebrows at her friend. Hannah grinned in return.

Liam was in the middle of a sentence, but as Hannah approached the table, he stopped and beamed a welcome at her. "Hi."

He had his arm resting across the back of the chair beside him. Did she need to ask if someone was sitting there? Hannah glanced at the chair and thought about what it would look like to the room if she sat beside him and he kept his arm there. Everyone would think they were dating, wouldn't they? And they were, kind of. Or they were trying to, anyway.

"I saved you a seat."

He didn't move his arm off the back of the chair, even though the Holt twins were watching. Even though they were in a room full of their friends. Even though keeping his arm there definitely made the two of them look as though they were something official.

"Thank you." Hannah flushed and took the seat. "I'm a few minutes later than I intended to be. Did I miss anything?"

She smiled across the table to greet Jacky and Alex, but her mind whirred with the awareness of Liam's arm draped behind her. He wasn't touching her, but if she allowed herself to lean back, to relax, they *would* be touching. It was as though he was offering yet leaving her the choice.

"Isaac is busy making fancy coffees," Alex said with an easygoing smile. Hannah had always liked him. "I'm sure he'll be out in a moment to get your order."

"Amelia talked about taking orders," Jacky added. There was a twinkle in her eye, likely about Hannah and Liam. "But then she decided that she wants opinions and feedback on everything, so she's basically bringing out all the food to everybody."

"If breakfast tastes half as good as it smells, I imagine my feedback will be 'this is delicious, and I want the recipe.'" Hannah said. "I should've worn pants with an elastic waistband."

"A grave mistake," Liam said from beside her, his voice a warm rumble.

Hannah turned to smile at him and was a little surprised by how close they were sitting. The other times they'd eaten together, they'd sat across the table from each other. This was new and... wonderful. She relaxed against the back of her seat and felt the warm press of Liam's arm against her shoulders. She tried not to beam, but she wasn't sure how well she did. And maybe it didn't matter, because Liam looked happy too.

"One dry cappuccino." Isaac stood beside their table and set a mug in front of Alex then another in front of Jacky as he said, "And one chai latte. Liam, yours is next. Hannah, what can I get you? Don't hold back on me. With our machine, I can make pretty much anything you can get at your favorite coffee shop, and I'd like the practice."

Hannah had never seen Isaac so enthusiastic, as if serving specialty coffees was the best job in the world. She wasn't used to thinking about coffee without the aid of a menu board. "I really don't know."

"I can make lattes, cappuccinos, americanos, macchiatos—you name it."

Hannah preferred brewed coffee with a sweet breakfast, but asking Isaac for that seemed almost insulting. Like going to a steakhouse and ordering chicken.

"How about an americano?" she finally said. It was fancier than brewed coffee but should give her a similar experience with breakfast.

"Excellent. Room for cream?"

"Uh, yes."

"I'll be right back."

Hannah watched Isaac stride across the dining room and through the door into the kitchen. She caught a glimpse of Amelia flipping something, and her own hands twitched with a sudden eagerness to help.

"I've never been so aggressively asked for my coffee order," Alex said as he placed his drink on the table. "But that's an excellent cappuccino."

"Apparently, that's what Isaac would like to do eventually," Jacky said as she sipped her drink. "Own a coffeehouse."

"Sounds like trouble for Zane," Liam said. His arm pressed against Hannah and made her stomach feel fluttery. Once she got some caffeine in her system, she might start bouncing around the dining room.

"Oh, I don't think Zane needs to be worried," Hannah said. "I don't think Isaac likes small-town life."

Jacky tilted her head. "Yeah. I've picked up on that too."

"I think owning a coffee shop sounds awful. Every morning is an early morning when you own a place like that, and I like my sleep." Alex rubbed at his short brown hair. "Anything in food service sounds terrible to me, actually. It's so much work."

"Alex." Jacky rolled her eyes. "Hannah is sitting right here. Could you at least pretend to worry about hurting her feelings?"

"Why would it hurt her feelings to know that her job looks so hard I wouldn't want to do it?" Alex grinned at Hannah. "Hannah knows I'm eternally grateful she's not as lazy as I am. Your brined pork chops with the homemade applesauce? Unbeatable."

"That's one of my favorites too," Hannah said, grinning.

"See?" Alex nudged his sister. "She's not offended. I'm glad people do things like open restaurants and coffeehouses. All I'm saying is, it seems like a lot of work."

Hannah chuckled. "And your job is so easy, Alex?"

He laughed and pushed his chair onto its back two legs, as if they were all sitting in a classroom together. "Absolutely. I make sure all the hard cases land on Jacky's desk."

Jacky cut a staged glare at her brother. "I knew it. I'm telling Colin to make sure you start pulling your weight around the station."

Alex laughed even harder and let his chair fall to the floor. He picked up his coffee and took another sip. "So good. I wonder if he and Sabrina Hill have gotten together. She was talking to me the other day about buying a hotel in Louisville that has a coffeehouse for sale next door."

Hannah startled. "Is she moving to Louisville? I hadn't heard that."

Alex shrugged.

"My brother knows all kinds of things like that," Jacky said in an annoyed voice. "People just *tell* him things. It's like a superpower."

"It's a natural reaction to my charisma, thank you very much." Alex leaned back in his chair again. He winked at Liam. "The uniform helps, right?"

Liam chuckled and shrugged. His hand was nearly resting on Hannah's shoulder now. She had to admit that she *did* like seeing Liam in his uniform, which was unfair because her chef's coat and toque were not flattering at all.

Amelia swept out of the kitchen holding an oversize serving tray, and Isaac followed close behind her with another one.

"Dylan would drop that for sure," Liam whispered in her ear.

Hannah stifled a laugh. She'd been thinking the same thing.

Amelia placed the serving trays on the sideboard, and then she turned to face her guests.

"My dear friends and neighbors." She paused, and her chin began to quiver.

Hannah's eyes felt misty. What a remarkable thing it was, to see a dream achieved right before her eyes. To watch Amelia push and push and push and finally arrive.

Amelia dabbed her eyes with the corner of her apron. "I was going to make a little speech, but I'm not sure I can get through it without crying."

"You don't need to make a speech," Isaac said.

He seemed embarrassed by his aunt's behavior, and Hannah felt a flush of annoyance. Hadn't Amelia earned the right to recognize the moment with a speech?

"Oh, you're probably right." Amelia ducked her head, looking flustered. "Besides, if I do that, the food will get cold and—"

"Speech!" Lacy called from her table.

Hannah grinned at her best friend. "Speech!" she and Liam called out simultaneously. The chant was taken up around the dining room.

Isaac shook his head, as if he couldn't believe this turn of events, but Amelia laughed.

"Okay, okay. Just a quick one." She drew in a long, deep breath. "I'm so grateful you're all here. Each one of you has played a part in Sally's opening. I know there was probably a time when each of us thought it wasn't going to happen, but thanks to all of you, Isaac and I were able to persevere, and we've finally reached today."

Hannah burst into applause and was immediately joined by others.

"Many of you knew my mother," Amelia went on, her chin still quivering. "Sally Jacobsen could be a challenging woman, especially in her final days. I inherited many things from her, but one of the most valuable gifts has been her stubbornness. She hoped that someday she'd be able to open a place like this, and it fills me with great joy that this day has come. I've asked Pastor Bob to say a blessing, and then Isaac and I will start passing out the food."

Pastor Bob stood from his seat and beamed at the room. "Let's all bow our heads."

With joy, Hannah bowed her head to give thanks to God for this remarkable moment in her friend's life.

Chapter Twenty-Two

Hannah had expected the food to be delicious, and she wasn't disappointed. Every bite was amazing. Amelia flitted about the dining room like a butterfly, chatting about ingredients and asking opinions while Isaac stayed busy with coffee orders.

"Where has stuffed French toast been my whole life?" Jacky asked as she helped herself to another piece. "I can't get over how wonderful this is. I've only had the kind that's just white bread dipped in eggs, and I thought I didn't like French toast. This has definitely changed my mind."

Hannah wished Amelia was standing with them and could hear Jacky's words, because hearing somebody say that now they actually *did* like a kind of food was one of the highest compliments a chef could receive. Hannah still grinned at the memory of teaching her dad that he enjoyed brussels sprouts—as long as she sautéed them in a little bacon grease and doused them in a lemon butter sauce.

Amelia stood at Lacy and Neil's table, speaking animatedly. "It's one of the most charming inns I've ever stayed in. And I'm not just saying that because a dear friend owns it. The two of you would love it." Amelia scanned the room until her gaze landed on her nephew. "Isaac, tell the Minyards they absolutely must stay at Goldenrod Inn when they're in Louisville."

Isaac grinned and made a chef's kiss with his fingers. "Yes, you must. And you must visit Grinders Coffeehouse next door. I go every time I stay at Goldenrod, and it's always the highlight."

"Oh." Amelia frowned as if she'd just remembered something. "Carol said that place is up for sale now."

Isaac looked away. "Really?"

"Yes, she said there's a big sign out front. I was surprised you didn't tell me after you'd been to Louisville. Carol said she spoke to the owner, and somebody put in an offer. I told her I wished the timing was different, because otherwise I was thinking you might be interested."

Isaac's laugh sounded tight as he turned away from his aunt and marched toward the kitchen, two empty coffee cups in hand. Hannah's gaze trailed after him.

An entire conversation was happening between the Holt twins and Liam. She brought her focus back to the table and attempted to reengage.

"I feel like the cost of adding a traffic light there is worth the expense," Alex was saying.

"Me too." Liam sipped at the dregs of his coffee. "We get called out there every week, it feels like."

Alex launched into a related story, and Hannah glanced at Jacky. She had a faraway look in her eye, like she was thinking of something else. Not a dreamy something else, like stuffed French toast. More like a concerning something else, judging from the lines furrowing her forehead.

Amelia moved over to their table holding a pan of fresh cinnamon rolls. "Caramel apple cinnamon roll?"

Liam shook his head. "Sounds amazing, but I couldn't eat another bite."

"I can." Alex patted his stomach. "I'll just start buying bigger pants."

Hannah had already eaten her fair share of stuffed French toast, sage sausage, and a three-cheese omelet, but she wasn't about to pass up a caramel apple cinnamon roll.

Jacky's concerned expression had vanished, and she eyed the pan with a mixture of longing and caution. "I'm so full, I think I can only eat half of one."

"I'll split one with you," Hannah said. "Everything is incredible, Amelia."

Amelia flashed a smile her way. "And within budget, you'll be happy to hear."

Hannah grinned. "That *is* good to hear, because I want Sally's to be profitable."

"And that wasn't going to happen with the type of menus I originally put together." Amelia shook her head then beamed at the Holt twins. "I'm so glad the two of you could make it. It's like having Sherlock Holmes come for breakfast, times two."

Jacky chuckled. "You're overstating our skills, Amelia."

"Maybe just yours," Alex said around a mouthful of cinnamon roll. "I'm Holmes, and you're Watson."

Jacky rolled her eyes at her brother, which made Hannah grin.

"Are you talking about Sherlock Holmes over there?" Neil called from several tables away.

"Oh no." Lacy shook her head, but her smile was pure affection. "I hope you wanted Neil at your table, because you won't get rid of him now."

"I've actually never read a Sherlock Holmes book," Alex admitted. "I've just seen the various TV shows over the years."

That was all the invitation Neil needed to hop up from his seat.

"You should read them." Amelia said. She added a cinnamon roll to Liam's plate despite his earlier protest. He winked at Hannah and reached for his fork. "Neil suggested that I start with the short stories, so that's what I've been reading at night before going to bed. I find mysteries that are solved quickly very calming."

"Alex, you should start with *The Memoirs of Sherlock Holmes*," Neil said. He stood beside the table, hands in his pockets. "It's a great short story collection."

"My favorite from that collection is 'The Adventure of Silver Blaze,'" Amelia said, looking as happy as Neil to be discussing Sherlock Holmes.

"Mine too." Neil deepened his voice and said in a horrible British accent, "'That was the curious incident.'"

Both Neil and Amelia laughed heartily. Hannah looked at Lacy, who smiled and shrugged.

When Amelia turned back to the table, she must have noticed their confused faces. "It's a line from the story."

"A famous line," Neil added. "You've probably heard it before. The curious incident of the dog in the night-time?"

"No," Alex dragged out the word. "I have no idea what you're talking about."

"Same here," Hannah and Jacky said simultaneously.

"Ditto," Liam added.

"Really?" Neil's eyes were wide with surprise. "Well, Sherlock says to the detective from Scotland Yard that he wants to talk about 'the curious incident of the dog in the night-time.' And the detective says the dog did nothing in the night-time, and Sherlock Holmes says, 'That was the curious incident.'"

Neil waited expectantly, reminding Hannah of a passionate English teacher she'd had who always wanted the class to be as enraptured by William Shakespeare as he was.

When no one responded, Neil pushed his glasses up the bridge of his nose. "It's because the dog barked at strangers but he didn't bark the night the horse was taken. *That's* what was curious. *That's* how he knew the culprit wasn't a stranger to the dog."

"I warned you not to get him going on Sherlock Holmes," Lacy called from the other table.

But in Hannah's mind, she was at the hostess stand, filling in for Elaine, and listening to Togo bark and bark and bark. Except when Isaac walked by. Not only had he not barked, but he'd actually wagged his tail. *Curious*, indeed.

"I think they know each other."

"What did you say, Hannah?" Amelia said.

Hannah hadn't realized she'd spoken aloud. "Nothing. This cinnamon roll is delicious. I wish I wasn't already so full."

As Amelia left the table to offer cinnamon rolls to the others who were probably all as stuffed as Hannah was, her thoughts drifted to what Sabrina had said about Isaac and Amelia arguing right before Amelia left town. And if she remembered correctly, Sabrina had stumbled around a bit when asked where she'd heard that. Isaac must have told Sabrina about the argument.

Then there was the time earlier in the week when Hannah was on the phone with Isaac, and a dog began barking. Isaac had hung up quickly after that. Was he worried she would recognize Togo's bark?

There was the jacket too. Sabrina had gotten road resurfacing material on her jacket, even though she'd said she hadn't been out of town since going to Michigan. Hannah had pushed her on that one, and Sabrina claimed it must have been from a guest's car. But how likely was that? As far as Hannah could tell, Sabrina's role at the hotel never placed her anywhere near guests' cars. Was the black substance actually from being around Isaac's SUV?

Why would Isaac try to help Sabrina though? He needed this job. Didn't he? Maybe Sabrina was paying Isaac to sabotage his aunt. Maybe he'd never gone to Louisville at all. Maybe he'd been here, robbing his aunt's safe. But there was the black substance on his car—

"Hannah, are you okay?" Jacky asked.

Hannah locked eyes with the deputy. "I'd like to talk to you. Somewhere private."

If Jacky was surprised, she didn't show it. She nodded and scooted away from the table.

"Is something wrong?" Liam asked as Hannah pushed her chair back as well.

"I don't know." Hannah tried to smile in a reassuring way but doubted she was successful. "I'll just be a moment."

Jacky wore a serious expression as the two of them slipped into the entryway near the front desk. Hannah glanced at the chairs where she and Amelia had sat on the morning of the robbery. Could Isaac have robbed Amelia while she was at church, driven far enough to Louisville to get asphalt on his car, and then driven back to create an alibi for himself? Louisville was only a few hours away, so it wasn't as though one needed to spend the night.

"What's wrong?" Jacky asked in a low voice.

Lacy came into the room. "What's going on?"

Hannah gave Lacy a tight smile, glad her friend had followed. "Maybe it's nothing."

But she knew it wasn't nothing. "It started when Amelia was telling Isaac that the coffee shop by Goldenrod Inn was for sale. His reaction struck me as odd." Hannah remembered the expression on Jacky's face after overhearing that conversation. "Maybe you thought it was odd too."

"Well." Jacky seemed to be debating whether she should say something. Finally, she said, "I'm probably a bit hyperaware because that's why Isaac was never considered a suspect. He was in Louisville. There was also the problem of motive. Why would he steal from his aunt and jeopardize his job?"

"I think I might have the answer to that," Hannah said slowly. "I think he and Sabrina are closer than they've let on."

Jacky's expression gave away nothing. "Go on."

Hannah hesitated a moment and then walked Jacky and Lacy through her thought process. What she'd observed that day at the hostess stand, when Togo had barked at every passing person except Isaac. About Sabrina's coat being stained with the substance used to resurface roads, even though she hadn't driven to Louisville, and how Isaac's wheel wells had been coated in the stuff when he came back. That Sabrina had mentioned to Hannah that Isaac and Amelia had argued before Amelia left, and then tried to play it off as town gossip.

When Hannah finished, Lacy made a humming sound. Then she said, "That could be why no *one* person fits the crimes. Because it's not one person. It's two people working together."

Jacky nodded. "Could be."

"Is something wrong?"

Amelia stood in the wide doorway of the room, concern knotted between her eyebrows. Her hair had the disheveled look characteristic of taking a hairnet on and off all morning as she moved between cooking and serving.

Hannah swallowed hard, hating the idea of bringing up Isaac's possible involvement today of all days. If Isaac really was involved in sabotaging the bed and breakfast, Amelia would be heartbroken.

"Amelia," Jacky said in a slow, even voice, "do the entire grounds belong to you?"

Amelia's gaze flicked from face to face, as if she was searching to understand the situation better. "Yes."

"What about the house Isaac lives in?"

Amelia's eyes widened. "Yes, all of it."

Jacky nodded. "Amelia, would you give Alex and me permission to search *everywhere* on the grounds for the items that were stolen from you?"

Amelia's mouth opened. She looked confused—but only for a moment. "It was Isaac, wasn't it?" Her voice had a breathy, almost distant sound to it, as if she wasn't really speaking to them. "All that talk about delaying the opening. And that serious conversation he had with me, trying to convince me that I should purchase Blackberry Inn instead of renovating Sally's. Of course it was him."

Hannah cast a sideways glance at Jacky, who watched Amelia with an interested expression but didn't seem eager to stop Amelia's verbal processing.

"And then that leak happened. I always thought he stopped it just in time, but maybe not. I came home earlier than I was supposed to, so maybe he had to change his plan. Make it look like he'd just discovered it, when really, he had caused it." Amelia's hands knotted in front of her. "And Mom's recipes were in that safe. Of course he wanted those. The secret ones weren't in there, but he didn't know that."

Hannah held her breath and prayed.

Amelia's mouth pressed into a grim line. Her focus sharpened on Jacky. "Go ahead. Search anywhere on the grounds you'd like."

Chapter Twenty-Three

While Jacky slipped away with Alex, Hannah quickly and quietly told Liam what was happening. She could see Lacy was doing the same with Neil. The two of them then moved to take the twins' spots at Hannah and Liam's table.

"How do you think we can help with the investigation?" Neil asked, clearly as delighted as if Sherlock Holmes himself had invited him to help with a case.

"Jacky told Amelia to act as though nothing was going on and to keep Isaac occupied," Hannah murmured.

At that moment, Isaac came into the dining room, carrying two mugs for Pastor Bob and Lorelai. As soon as he'd delivered them, Hannah called over, "Isaac, Lacy really enjoyed the latte you made for her. Would you mind making one for me?"

Isaac sauntered over to their table, beaming. "Caramel latte, right?"

"That's right," Lacy said. "So good. What's your secret?"

"The espresso matters, of course. I won't even tell you how many types of espresso I tried before selecting this one." Isaac crossed his arms over his chest. Hannah had never seen someone manage to look so smug while wearing a waist apron. "But with the flavored drinks, the syrup brand makes all the difference. I mentioned that to Zane earlier because he was on my case about how our syrup is twice as expensive as what he uses at Jump Start."

The thought made the restaurateur inside Hannah cringe. "But you won't even charge guests for your coffees here," she pointed out.

"That's right." Isaac nodded. "Just a perk of being a guest at Sally's. It's not all about cutting costs, Hannah. Quality matters too."

"Well, sure it does, but—"

"I'll take one of those caramel lattes too," Liam interjected. "If you don't mind. I want to taste for myself what all the fuss is about."

"All right. I'll be back."

When he'd exited the dining room, Liam gave Hannah an apologetic look. "I just figured we don't need to get him all stirred up about quality and cost." He jerked his head toward the kitchen. "That man is childish enough to go stomping off to his room in a rage."

"I should've reviewed the inventory for the coffee bar too." Hannah bit her lip. "Amelia said Isaac was taking care of that part, and he didn't ask for my help, of course. But it was all coming out of Amelia's budget, so I really should've—"

"Hannah," Lacy said gently, "I think after this morning it's going to be a moot point."

Hannah thought her friend was right, but still. "Well, if we're wrong about him being involved in what's been going on around here, I'm going to have a conversation with Amelia."

Hannah was bursting to talk more about Isaac, to ask if there were other connections to Sabrina that any of them might have noticed, but she knew it was a bad idea while sitting in Sally's dining room.

Once again, Liam saved her. "How's it going at Legend and Key?" he asked Neil.

They carried on with small talk for a few minutes before Amelia's sharp voice cut through the din of chatter in the dining room. "How could you?"

The four of them at the table exchanged glances then jumped up and rushed into the kitchen. Hannah skidded to a halt at the sight of Jacky and Alex holding evidence bags containing a wooden box, jewelry, and cash. Isaac stood red-faced beside his beloved espresso machine, and Amelia glared at him.

"Everybody said that I was making a mistake by bringing you into the business," Amelia continued. "Even your mother worried that it was a bad idea."

"I—" Isaac swallowed. "I don't know how those got in my room. I mean, I was in Louisville during the robbery. It couldn't have been me."

Amelia continued to glare at her nephew in silence.

Isaac swallowed again. "Carol will tell you that's where I was. She saw me check in at Goldenrod Inn. So, um, I don't know how those got in my room, but they must have been planted there, because it couldn't have been me."

"But it could've been Sabrina." Hannah swallowed hard when the others swiveled their heads to look at her. "Because the two of you were working together."

Hannah knew from the way Isaac's eyes widened and the way his cheeks flushed a deeper shade of red that she'd guessed right. "N-no, I barely know her." His protest rang hollow.

"You're the one person her dog doesn't bark at. And that black substance that was all over your car when you got back from Louisville is also on her jacket."

Isaac made a snorting sound. "A dog that doesn't bark? Tar on her jacket? That's all you've got?"

"That," Jacky said, "and the fingerprints."

Isaac turned slowly to Jacky, his expression one of dread.

"There are multiple prints on these." Alex held up a bag of jewelry and the bag with the recipe box. "We'll get these and you and Sabrina down to the station and see if they match."

Jacky cocked her head to the side and studied Isaac. "And I bet her prints are in your car too. We'll have to get a search warrant to find out for sure, but it shouldn't be too hard to do now that we've found the stolen items in your room."

Isaac stared at the floor, as if hoping it would swallow him up and he could escape.

"Or," Amelia said in a voice that was sad yet firm, "instead of going through all that, you can come clean and tell me now. Why'd you do it, Isaac?"

Isaac said nothing. A muscle in his jaw ticked.

"The way I figure it," Amelia continued, "Sabrina was angry that I wouldn't buy Blackberry Inn. Maybe she thought if things were bad enough here, I'd give up and walk away from renovating Mom's place. But how'd she talk you into helping?"

"You think you're so smart, don't you?" Isaac grumbled.

"Being disrespectful isn't going to help you right now," Liam told him.

"Was the water leak you too?" Amelia pressed, apparently unconcerned about Isaac's attitude. "You told me you had errands to run that morning. I remember now that when I pulled in the driveway, I was surprised to see you were already back. When I came in and you said there was a leak, I thought it was a blessing that you'd come home when you did, but now..."

"Sabrina was out of town during the water leak." Lacy glanced at Hannah. "That's why we ruled her out."

"Right." Hanah nodded. "And then for the robbery, Isaac was out of town. But he could have told Sabrina the combination and had her hide everything in his room, in case her place was searched."

Isaac glared at Hannah.

"Is that right, Isaac?" Amelia prompted.

A long silence stretched, and then Isaac said, "I'm not saying anything without a lawyer present."

"Oh, Isaac," Amelia said with an exasperated groan, "I'm your *aunt*. You don't need a lawyer."

He looked at her, his chin raised defiantly.

"You *don't*," Amelia insisted. "I just want you to tell me the truth. Even if you were helping Sabrina. Even if you caused the leak and assisted in the robbery, I just want to *know*. I'm not going to press charges."

Alex made a sound in his throat as if he wanted to interrupt, but Amelia ignored him.

"Just tell me the truth," Amelia said again, peering into her nephew's eyes. "Can't you show me enough respect to at least do that?"

Isaac dragged in a deep breath. "The truth? The truth is that I hate this town. I hate being where I can't start a coffeehouse because somebody else already did and there's no space for another one. I hate that everywhere I go, I'm Amelia's nephew or Sally's grandson. That's all I get to be when I'm here. The relative of two women who don't even care enough about me to tell me how to make the special family recipes. The recipes are too precious to entrust to me, apparently. Even though I'm a Jacobsen, same as you."

"Oh, Isaac," Amelia said again, more softly this time, "I bet you were disappointed when they weren't in the box, weren't you? I would've taught the recipes to you if you'd ever cared enough to work alongside me in the kitchen. That's how the special ones get passed down, with time together."

Isaac looked away from his aunt.

Amelia took a deep breath. "Like I said, I'm not going to press charges, but you do need to move out. Right away. And obviously, you no longer work here."

Isaac sneered at his aunt. "You don't have to ask me twice. I'm happy to leave."

"But I'd advise you to stick around town for the next few days," Jacky added. "We'll have more questions for you after we talk to Sabrina."

Isaac stormed out the back door, slamming it hard behind him. Thirty seconds later, his SUV roared to life, and gravel crunched loudly under his tires.

"Let's go," Alex said to his sister. "I don't want him getting to Sabrina before we do."

The two of them took off, leaving Hannah, Liam, Lacy, Neil, and Amelia standing in the silent kitchen.

Chapter Twenty-Four

"Well," Amelia said in a small, wavery voice. She gave Hannah a weak smile. "I guess that solves the mystery, doesn't it?"

And the woman who had endured so much over the last few months began to cry.

Hannah crossed the kitchen to her friend and wrapped her in a hug. "I'm so sorry."

"I'm fine. I really am," Amelia sobbed. "I'm sad of course, but it's also a relief. An answer to prayer."

"An answer to prayer?" Liam repeated. "How so?"

Amelia stepped back from the hug and wiped her eyes with her apron. "When I was away, I told God that I didn't want to open Sally's not knowing who was set against me. Of course I'm disappointed to learn that it was Isaac, but being disappointed is better than not knowing. And honestly, I feel more hopeful about the future of Sally's now than I have in months."

Hannah's heart lifted. With her own eyes, she was witnessing an example of the verse in Romans, that suffering produced perseverance, which produced character, which produced hope.

Hannah's eyes blurred with tears. "Amelia, you're amazing. The way you've persevered through this whole situation has taught me so much."

"It's taught all of us," Lacy said, linking her arm through Neil's.

"I can't believe you're still opening today," Liam added.

"The first guests will arrive in a few hours." Amelia smiled. "I'm really excited about that. All I've wanted this whole time is to welcome people to my home and feed them good food."

Hannah grinned and gave Amelia a side hug. "Good news, friend. Today is the day."

Amelia beamed back at Hannah and echoed, "Today is the day."

The four of them stayed to help Amelia clean up the kitchen and reset the dining room, so they were all still there when Jacky and Alex returned, carrying the evidence bags once more. The grins on their faces as they came into the kitchen told Hannah that the interview had been successful, even before they said as much.

"That girl melted so fast," Alex told them. "As soon as we confronted her, she told us everything."

Jacky placed the evidence bags on the kitchen counter and said to Amelia, "You can have these back. We should be done with them."

"What did you learn?" Amelia asked.

"Sabrina confirmed she and Isaac were working together. She made it sound like it was all his idea." Jacky cocked her head, as though considering this. "We're not sure whether that's true or not."

Hannah had her doubts too. She remembered the afternoon when she observed Togo not barking at Isaac and the way Sabrina had smiled at him as he'd passed by.

"She said she had nothing to do with the water leak. That was entirely Isaac," Alex continued.

Amelia frowned.

"Again," Jacky cut in, "Sabrina could be trying to spin the story in her favor, but it's true that nothing ever linked her to that event.

She wasn't even in town. And she was very up front about what happened with the safe. She said she waited until you went to church. Then she opened the safe and put the things in Isaac's room at his request."

"If you want to press charges, Amelia, we can help with that." Alex leaned against the counter, his arms crossed over his chest. "Although it's a little tricky, seeing as the stolen items never left the grounds and the person who 'broke in' walked through an unlocked door and used the combination."

"I didn't even know they knew each other," Amelia murmured.

"That was intentional." Another voice cut into the conversation.

Hannah whirled to find Sabrina standing in the doorway of the kitchen looking absolutely miserable. She was still the put-together woman, with smooth hair and high heels, but her face had an openness about it that Hannah had never seen before.

Sabrina glanced around the room, and then her gaze settled on Amelia. "I'm sorry to intrude. I imagine I'm the last person you want to see right now, but I had to come over and try to explain myself."

Hannah thought Amelia could handle whatever Sabrina had to say, with the way her shoulders squared and her spine straightened.

"Go ahead," Amelia said.

"Isaac and I met soon after he moved here. We were waiting for our coffee orders at Jump Start, and he brought up Grinder's in Louisville. We bonded quickly because I've always loved the Goldenrod Inn—that was my inspiration for the remodel plans at Blackberry—and Isaac mentioned that it might be for sale soon."

Sabrina inhaled deeply and adjusted her gaze so she was looking at the floor instead of Amelia. "A few days later, he reached out and told me that opening Sally's was a bigger job than you'd counted on. He was certain you would be interested in buying Blackberry Inn from me instead and that it could work out well for everyone. I believed him because I hadn't yet met Amelia." She gave Amelia a pleading expression. "I thought you would prefer to own a historic hotel that *wasn't* as big a job as this place, and that I would be able make an offer on Goldenrod and have the kind of hotel I wanted in a city rather than here."

"And you thought Isaac was arranging this out of the goodness of his heart?" Liam asked.

Sabrina nodded. "I understand if you don't believe me, Chief Berthold, but Isaac was very charming." Her face flushed. "I thought he was interested in me and trying to create a life for us in Louisville, as well as look out for his aunt."

"I know he can be very charming," Amelia said slowly. "My sister-in-law—his mother—warned me about that when I offered him the job. I told her that I used to change his diapers and I was therefore immune to being charmed by him. I didn't think about the fact that others might not be immune."

"Why did you keep your relationship a secret?" Hannah asked.

"We both agreed on that, actually," Sabrina said. "Last year when I was seeing someone and we broke up, I couldn't go anywhere in town without some well-meaning person giving me a hug, or telling me how sorry they were, or how they had known all along that it was never going to work out. I really didn't want to go through that again. And I guess Isaac had his own reasons. I just didn't realize it at the time."

Sabrina released a gusty sigh. "I got carried away by the dream of it all, honestly. I envisioned my future with Isaac, where he owned

Grinder's and I owned Goldenrod. My parents would be thrilled to have Blackberry Inn belong to somebody who wanted to preserve the original 1940s look. And I even told myself that you would be happier in the long run too, Amelia. I got so carried away that I convinced myself I wasn't *really* doing anything wrong by breaking into your safe like Isaac asked. He'd given me the code, and I was simply relocating the stuff to his room. The belongings were staying on the grounds, with the family. I told myself I wasn't stealing. I was just hiding those things from you."

Sabrina shook her head, seemingly at herself. "Amelia, I know this doesn't change anything, but I am *so* sorry about what happened and my involvement with the whole situation. As I've watched you restore this place, it's made me rethink how I view Blackberry Inn. It's helped me to see that the building has its own history that I need to honor rather than trying to make it into something it isn't."

"Oh, child." Amelia opened her arms and folded Sabrina into a hug.

"I'm so sorry," Sabrina said again, voice breaking. "If you want to press charges, I understand. It's what I deserve."

Amelia shook her head. "I have no interest in doing that. Everything was returned to me, and all I want to do now is get this place ready for my guests."

Hannah wasn't surprised at all by Amelia's reaction. Or that she sent Sabrina home with the rest of the caramel apple cinnamon rolls.

After Sabrina left, the officers hung out for a few more minutes, chatting with Amelia about adding some security cameras to the property and changing the locks in the doors of the gardener's house. After that, they said goodbye and left with a box of rosemary lemon shortbread, toffees, and more specialty treats from Sally's.

"We'll get out of your way," Lacy told Amelia. "I know you have a lot to do."

"I do have a gift for you." Hannah reached into the pocket of her sweater to pull out the small jewelry box. "Just a little something to commemorate your opening day."

"This is completely unnecessary. You've already done so much," Amelia said, even as she lifted the lid off the box. "Oh, I love it." She removed the necklace from its pillow and held it up for the others to see.

Liam squinted at it. "Is it a...jackhammer?"

Hannah laughed. "A jackhammer?"

His eyes sparkled. "That's what it looks like to me."

"Why would I give Amelia a necklace with a jackhammer on it?"

"Because she's jackhammered her way through all the obstacles to get to this day." Liam raised his eyebrows at her. "Pretty good, right?"

"Looks like a rolling pin to me," Lacy said.

Hannah grinned. "And that's why we're best friends."

"A rolling pin?" Liam snorted. "It's a jackhammer. You're with me on this, right, Neil?"

"Oh, for sure." Neil nodded. "Definitely a jackhammer."

"It can be both." Amelia slipped the necklace over her head and patted the pendant where it rested on her chest. "I've needed both a rolling pin and a jackhammer to open Sally's." Her gaze rested on Hannah. "And friends. I've also needed friends."

Each of them gave Amelia one more hug. They headed out the front door, loaded down with their own boxes of goodies. Lacy and Neil waved goodbye and then held hands on their way to Lacy's truck.

Hannah wasn't in a hurry to leave Liam's side, and he didn't seem eager either. She drew her coat tighter around herself as she watched Lacy and Neil drive away. "I can't believe how at peace Amelia is with opening today. It's amazing, isn't it?"

"Incredible," Liam agreed, smiling down at her. "But not surprising. She's lucky to have a friend like you, who has worked so hard to help her start off on the right foot."

Hannah bit her lower lip. "I wish I'd put it together sooner. About Isaac and Sabrina, I mean."

"You still did it though. And I know it was uncomfortable for Amelia, but it also seems like the best Christmas present you could've given her—truth and peace."

Hannah took in a breath and exhaled slowly. "Which reminds me that Christmas is just three days away, and I still have so much left to do."

"I do too." Liam tucked his hands into his coat pockets "Plus work is always hectic this time of year. More people on the roads, more bad weather, more space heaters set too close to very dry Christmas trees."

"The restaurant will be busy too. We'll be closed Christmas Eve and Christmas Day, but those won't be particularly restful with all the family festivities. It's all fun stuff, of course. I just..."

I just want to have time to go on a date with you.

Could she say it as plain as that?

She looked into Liam's eyes and took a deep breath. "I just wish there was more time...for us." Hannah swallowed and looked away. "It seems like we're having such a hard time finding space in our calendars for each other. I keep telling myself it's because it's December and we're both busy."

She braved a glance up at his face and found him regarding her with solemn brown eyes. "That *is* why," he said. "It's entirely why. What else could it be?"

Hannah scuffed the toe of her boot on the ground. "When I first moved to LA, I went on a few dates with this guy, but they were all weeks or even a month apart from each other. I thought that was because we were both really busy, but then I realized it was actually because he didn't like me that much."

"No offense intended, but he doesn't sound like a very smart guy," Liam said, his voice warm.

Hannah felt the burn of her cheeks. "I just wasn't his type."

"I'm glad you weren't," Liam said. "In the past, I've had a hard time making space for a relationship with the erratic hours of my job and everything. But I've also never cared about someone the way I care about you. You've become important to me, Hannah, and I'd like to start treating you that way. I'd also like to start introducing you to other people that way—as my girlfriend. Is that all right?"

Joy bloomed in Hannah's chest. "I would love that, Liam."

Liam grinned. "I know this month has been really challenging for both of us, but will you please give me your phone?"

Had she heard him wrong? "My phone?"

He held out his hand. "Yes, your phone."

"Uh, okay."

She did as he asked, and Liam tapped away on her phone, careful to keep the screen turned so she couldn't see. "The twenty-eighth is your birthday, right?"

"Yeah."

"What if—and if you don't want to or you have other plans, I completely understand—but what if I took you to dinner that night?"

Her breath caught in her lungs. She could see in Liam's eyes that he knew this wasn't like asking for a random date. Choosing to spend the evening of her birthday with him was important, and Hannah knew there was nobody she would rather spend her birthday with.

"There's nothing I'd like more," she said with a grin.

"Good." Liam handed her phone back. "How's this look?"

Hannah took the phone from him and felt a flush of happiness all the way down to her toes. No longer did Liam's contact information say "Champion Chauffeur," but rather "Best Boyfriend."

She beamed up at him. "That's perfect."

He grinned back at her. "I'm glad we agree. And I'm glad we persevered to get here."

"Me too, Liam." Hannah said with a sigh. "Me too."

From the Author

Dear Reader,

After I became an adult, my parents, who were near retirement age, decided to open a coffeehouse in their community. While they had started several successful businesses over the years, they'd never done anything in food service, and watching them take on the adventure was equal parts fun and nerve-racking. (And delicious! It was often delicious!)

Because of that experience, I was eager to explore life in Blackberry Valley through Hannah's eyes as she balances running a successful restaurant with all the other challenges of life. Something I admired about my parents' decision was that—much like Amelia Jacobsen—as they were reaching a phase in life where they were "supposed to" be slowing down, they instead paid attention to the dream that was knocking on their hearts. I pray that I follow their example and never use my age as an excuse to not pursue dreams.

Wishing you a wonderful Christmas season,
Stephanie Coleman

About the Author

Stephanie Coleman is the author of several contemporary young adult series, as well as two historical young adult novels. Since 2010, Stephanie has been encouraging the next generation of writers at her website, GoTeenWriters.com, which has been on the Writer's Digest Best Websites for Writers list since 2017. She lives in the Kansas City area, where she loves plotting big and small adventures to enjoy with her husband and three children.

The Hot Spotlight

Famous Secret Recipes

Around Christmastime, there are often jokes about nobody really liking fruitcake, but my dad and his two brothers were obsessed with my grandmother's. They raved about it year round, they eagerly anticipated it all year long, and they waxed poetic during the holiday season when Nana finally baked and served it. Her fruitcake was apparently light and fruity perfection, but Nana wouldn't share the recipe. Not even with family. She kept the recipe to herself until she was in her eighties and moved in with my parents.

When creating the character of Sally Jacobsen, I thought about my grandmother, and I became interested in the idea of recipes that are kept secret.

The most famous example is Coca-Cola. The soft drink was invented in 1886 by a pharmacist in Atlanta and its composition is still, reportedly, a handwritten formula on a piece of paper. The company holds the recipe in a secure vault at their headquarters.

If you're a fan of Huy Fong Sriracha, you know that it has a unique taste from other hot sauces. Originally created in a small town in Thailand called Si Racha, the recipe itself isn't the big secret. Rather the specialized machinery and a unique production process create a taste that can't be replicated by others.

KFC guards Colonel Sanders's recipe for fried chicken within two-foot-thick walls and twenty-four-hour surveillance. The recipe was developed in the 1940s, and only two KFC executives know every herb and spice used in their unique formula.

Keeping a recipe secret for the sake of protecting your business makes sense, but if I'm lucky enough to bake something special at Christmas that my kids eagerly await all year long, I will certainly hand them the recipe!

From the Hot Spot Kitchen

ROSEMARY LEMON SHORTBREAD

Ingredients:

2 cups all-purpose flour

⅔ cup granulated sugar

1 tablespoon fresh rosemary, finely chopped

2 tablespoons lemon zest, freshly grated

1 teaspoon kosher salt

1 cup salted butter, cut into chunks

Directions:

Preheat oven to 325 degrees. Pulse together flour, sugar, rosemary, lemon zest, and salt in food processor. Add butter and pulse to fine crumbs. Pulse a few more times until some crumbs come together, but don't overprocess. Dough will not be smooth.

Press dough into ungreased 8x8- or 9x9-inch square baking pan or 9-inch pie plate. Prick dough all over with fork and bake until golden brown, 35 to 40 minutes for 9-inch pan and 45 to 50 minutes for 8-inch.

After removing from oven, allow to cool for a bit, then cut into squares, bars, or wedges while still warm. Enjoy!

Read on for a sneak peek of another exciting book in the *Mysteries of Blackberry Valley* series!

Smoke and Mirrors

BY LAURA BRADFORD

"Am I the only one wishing Hannah could see just how big her smile is right now?"

Hannah Prentiss beamed at Lacy Minyard, who sat beside her at the head of a long table covered in a bright red cloth. Friends from all over Blackberry Valley lined the sides.

"I don't need to see it." Hannah grabbed hold of Lacy's hand and squeezed. "I feel it deep in my soul, thanks to you. You pulled off the perfect surprise birthday party."

Lacy's hazel eyes twinkled with joy.

Her hand still on her best friend's, Hannah took in each face to her left and to her right. "And thanks to all of you as well. You've made me feel very special this afternoon. Thank you for that, for your friendship, and for being exactly who you are. In fact, it's because of all of you that I had to think so long before blowing out my candles. I mean, what's left to wish for when I feel like I already have everything I could possibly want?"

"Like this restaurant," suggested Connie Sanchez, the church secretary and a fellow member of the monthly lunch group. She waved a hand at the empty tables and memorabilia-clad walls of the former firehouse-turned-eatery. "Which has become a real treasure in this town, I must say."

"I couldn't agree more," Sally Wright chimed in from her spot beside Connie. "My husband, who used to grouse at the mere suggestion of ever eating anywhere other than home, is now the one lobbying for us to come here to the Hot Spot at least once a week." She grinned. "So *I* must thank *you*, for *that*."

Hannah sank back in her chair and gazed around at the manifestation of her lifelong dream. Yes, the handful of tables beyond the one they used were empty at the moment, but she also knew that would change in a little over twenty-four hours.

"There's that smile again."

She met Lacy's gaze. "What can I say? I'm happy. The restaurant, being back in Blackberry Valley with Dad, Uncle Gordon, and my brother and his family, getting to see *you* again practically every day." She gestured to the women around the table. "And the kind of friends who would surprise me by turning what I thought was our normal ladies' luncheon for the month of January into a belated birthday party for me. I'm so blessed. Truly."

"And don't forget a certain—and rather handsome, I might add—fire chief you've reportedly been seen with around town a number of times this past week."

Her cheeks warming at the mere mention of Liam Berthold, Hannah swung her focus to the newest member of the ladies' luncheon group, Deputy Jacky Holt.

Jacky pantomimed pulling a notebook from the pocket of the police uniform she wasn't actually wearing and poised an imaginary pen above it. "What can you tell us about that, Ms. Prentiss?"

"Inquiring minds want to know, dear." Connie leaned forward in her spot opposite the off-duty deputy, as did Vanessa Lodge, the police department's young receptionist, and Miriam Spencer, the group's oldest member.

"There's really nothing to tell," Hannah said, only to stop at Lacy's answering snort.

Connie looked at Jacky. "Is that true?" she teased. "There's nothing to tell?"

Jacky grinned. "There have been reports."

"Oh?" Hannah drew back. "What kind of reports?"

"One citizen reported quiet laughter between you and the fire chief over lattes at Jump Start Coffee one afternoon this past week."

Hannah felt her brow lift, and she pointed at Vanessa. "Tattletale."

"Another mentioned bacon being hand-delivered to you here during a meeting with your staff one day last week," Jacky said across the top of her imaginary notebook.

Hannah shot a mock glare at Raquel Holden. Her waitress looked up and away, whistling innocently.

"And another reported a moonlit walk the two of you might have taken after Hot Spot hours Friday night."

Hannah's answering laugh mingled with Lacy's as she turned her attention to the town librarian, Evangeline Cooke. "I seem to remember passing you and Ted that night. In front of the market. You were walking your dog."

"The way he looked at you while you were talking." Evangeline set her fork and knife on her empty plate and met Hannah's gaze with a sheepish one of her own. "I couldn't *not* notice."

Jacky chuckled. "I'm just teasing you, Hannah. You don't have to tell us anything you don't want to."

"Yes, she does," Miriam huffed.

Laughter erupted around the table. Hannah waved her hand. "Fine. Okay. Yes. Liam and I have gone on a few—"

"They're officially dating," Lacy interrupted. "*Finally*, I might add."

Hannah watched the exchange of knowing looks and smiles taking place around her before she rose to her feet. "Liam and I are both very busy people, but, yes, we've decided to see how it goes."

"It's going to go wonderfully." Lacy started to stand and then sank back down, gripping the edge of the table as she did. "Whoa. That'll teach me not to get up so fast after two pieces of birthday cake."

Taking in her friend's suddenly pasty pallor, Hannah poured her a glass of water. "Here. Drink this. Don't get up until you're ready."

"But I want to help clean up," Lacy argued.

"And I want you to stay sitting." Hannah reached for her plate and Lacy's only to get her hand gently swatted away by Connie.

"Put that down right now, dear. You're the birthday girl, remember?"

"Technically, my birthday was two weeks ago."

"But we're celebrating it with you today."

"And I thank you for that, but the party is over," Hannah said, reaching for the plate once again.

"Hannah Prentiss!" Miriam scolded. "Respect your elders."

"I—"

The eighty-five-year-old met Hannah's wide eyes with a wink. She indicated the pile of opened presents on the chair between them. "We'll take care of the table *and* Lacy. You take these up to your apartment before I help myself to that apple-pie-scented candle Evangeline gave you and Jacky has to arrest me."

Hannah opened her mouth to protest, but Vanessa and Jacky each gathered up a few of the gifts, leaving Hannah with an armful of her own.

"Come on," Jacky said to her. "Vanessa and I will help you get these things up to your place, where you will remain until everything down here is cleaned up and back to normal."

"Are you sure?" Hannah asked. "I know *you're* off today, Jacky, but Vanessa—"

"Sheriff Steele okayed an extended lunch hour so I could be here for this." Vanessa checked the clock on the wall. "I have enough time to help get these upstairs before I need to head to the station."

With the help of her cane, Miriam rose to her feet, her attempt at another scowl hindered by the sparkle in her eyes. "Then it's settled. Hannah, shoo!"

Hannah planted a kiss on the elderly woman's cheek, returned the parade of hugs from the other women, instructed Lacy to wait to leave until she felt better, and then turned and led Vanessa and Jacky toward the steps to her apartment.

"Hannah, wait!"

She glanced over her shoulder to see Raquel hurrying in her direction with a wrapped gift in her hand.

"Raquel, you already gave me a gift," she protested.

"I know." Raquel set the box on top of the stack in Hannah's arms. "This one isn't from me."

Hannah looked down at the box and her name written on the tag beside the bow and then back up at her friend. "Then who is it from?"

Raquel shrugged. "I can't say for sure, but I did catch a glimpse of that girl outside the door as we were finishing up with the cake and presents. Maybe it was from her."

"Girl? What girl?"

"The reporter who works with Marshall over at the paper."

"Pippa Nelson?" Hannah frowned at the box. "I've left messages for her at the *Chronicle* before every one of our monthly luncheons, but she never comes. So how would she know this one was a belated birthday celebration for me if even *I* didn't know?"

"I think Evangeline saw her out and about sometime last week and mentioned it to her."

"She didn't have to get me a gift," Hannah protested.

"*If* it's from her at all," Raquel said. "There isn't a card that I can see, but maybe it's inside the box."

"Maybe." She smiled. "Thanks, Raquel."

"My pleasure, boss. And don't worry about things down here. I'll make sure Lacy is okay and that everything is locked up before we leave."

"I can come back down and lock up."

"Don't. We've got it covered. I promise." Raquel motioned toward the table that was already cleared. Connie was sweeping, under the audible supervision of Miriam. "Staff meeting tomorrow at two, right?"

"Right."

"I'll be there."

Hannah grinned. "I know you will. And probably fifteen minutes early, as usual."

"What can I say?" Raquel asked. "Punctuality was a big deal in my house growing up."

"Punctuality, diligence, positive attitude, et cetera, et cetera."

Her cheeks tinged red, Raquel waved aside Hannah's assessment. "You should stop before my head gets too big to fit through the doors around here."

"I just call it like I see it, my friend." Hannah resumed her trek toward the back of the restaurant and the two young women waiting for her at the bottom of the steps. "Sorry, guys. I was waylaid by another present."

"Oh, who from?" Jacky asked. "You already got one from everyone who was here today."

"Raquel thinks it might be from Pippa Nelson over at the paper, but she's not sure, and there doesn't appear to be a card."

"Perhaps Jacky can dust it for fingerprints," Vanessa teased as she followed Hannah and her coworker to the former fire station's second floor.

"I have the day off, remember?" Jacky volleyed back. "Unlike you, Vanessa. The sheriff is probably getting antsy about you being gone so long."

Vanessa's laugh followed Hannah inside her apartment. "Do you see what I have to put up with working with this one, Hannah? Bossy, bossy, bossy."

When everyone was inside the tiny entryway, Hannah pushed the door closed with her elbow and led her two friends into her cozy living room. "You can leave everything on the coffee table. I'll have to decide where it's all going."

"Roger that." Jacky set down her stack of gifts. "This was really fun today. I'm glad you talked me into joining the group, Hannah."

"I am too." She took a few steps toward the door but stopped when she realized neither woman was following her. "Are you all coming?"

Jacky and Vanessa shook their heads.

Hannah glanced at her watch and then up at Vanessa. "Don't you have to go?"

"I do."

At a loss for what to say, Hannah slid her attention onto Jacky and waited.

"We want to see what's in the mystery box," Jacky said.

"Right. Of course." Hannah sat on the couch and made short work of the tape to reveal a plain white box. Carefully, she opened the lid—and drew in her breath at the sight of what was inside. "Oh. Wow. This is *beautiful*."

Jacky folded her arms. "I don't do suspense all that well. I'm just saying."

Hannah carefully extracted the contents, a tiny creamer.

A gasp pulled her attention from the gift to Vanessa in time to see the young woman surge toward her with wide eyes. Before Hannah could process what was happening, Vanessa plucked the creamer from her hands and turned it over. "I—I don't understand. How do you have this? Where did it come from?"

Confused, Hannah dug her hand inside the box, moved the tissue paper around, and then shrugged. "I don't know. There's no note. Why?"

"I know this piece, I know the set it was part of!" Still clearly stunned, Vanessa looked from the creamer in her hands to Hannah and back again. "Many years ago, my grandmother was the cook at the Taylor Estate. The job came with a small cottage on the property where she and my grandaddy raised my mama. Grandma Peggy made pottery when she wasn't working at the main house, and Mama loved to watch. She said her mother would get up before dawn to work at her wheel and sometimes, when she was working on a new piece, she would stay up all night. But as busy as she was with that and cooking for the Taylors, Mama said Grandma Peggy still made time for her and that she had a way of making every moment they spent together special. They'd garden together, have fancy little tea parties in the cottage, lie on the grass at night and look up at the stars. All sorts of things."

Vanessa turned the creamer over in her hands again, her voice thick with emotion. "One day, when Mama was getting ready to move out on her own, Grandma Peggy surprised her with a whole dining set she'd made—dinner plates, dessert plates, candlesticks, a butter dish, a sugar bowl, and this creamer. Mama cried when she saw it because she knew how hard it must have been for Grandma Peggy to find the time to make all those pieces, what with working at the main house, caring for her family, and making all those other pieces she sold at the market on Saturday mornings."

"Your grandmother sounds like she was a wonderful person," Hannah said.

"She was." Vanessa ran her fingers along the twilight-blue glazed creamer and around its brown rim. "A few days later, Mama packed it all up and moved to her own little place. But when she went to unpack, she noticed this piece was missing."

"Wait." Hannah said, drawing back. "She hasn't seen it since her mother gave it to her?"

Vanessa turned over the creamer and pointed at a tiny rose etched into the bottom. "Grandma Peggy put her initials—*PSW*—on the bottom of all the pieces she sold. But on the ones she made for my mama, she put a rose to represent Mama's name. That set has been on Mama's table for every holiday and special occasion since. Well, minus this creamer and the sugar bowl, of course."

"Sugar bowl?"

Again, Vanessa nodded. "It went missing the same time this piece did."

"I don't understand," Hannah said. "Where has the creamer been this whole time, and who's giving it to me now after all these years? And where is the sugar bowl?"

"I don't know. Mama always said the only thing that made any sense was that it was stolen, but—" Vanessa looked down at her pocket and then handed the creamer to Hannah so she could check a text on her phone. "It's the station. I really should get back."

Jacky held up her own phone. "I just got a text too. Seems there's some sort of situation in Cave City, and they're looking for backup from our department. I'm going to head over there with Vanessa and see if I can do anything to help."

"Of course." Hannah stood, waited for Vanessa to type a response to whoever had texted her, and then held out the creamer. "Take this. Please."

"But it was given to you," Vanessa argued.

"It was, but it sounds like the person who should have it is your mother, not me."

Vanessa's dark eyes moved between the creamer and Hannah. "Are you sure?"

"I am."

"I—I don't know what to say. I can't believe we've found this. I really can't." Vanessa took the creamer and drew it to her chest as a smile spread across her face. "Thank you, Hannah. Mama is going to be so tickled."

A siren sounded on the street below. Hannah followed Vanessa and Jacky toward the door. "Thank you both for today. It was very special."

"It was." Vanessa and Jacky both hugged Hannah then hurried down the stairs.

When they were out of sight, Hannah closed the door then wandered back into the living room and over to the tissue-paper-filled box sitting on the coffee table. Sinking onto the sofa, she again searched it for any sign of a note or card, but to no avail.

"Where did you come from?" she whispered. "And why now? Why for me?"

Loved *Mysteries of Blackberry Valley?*
Check out some other Guideposts mystery series!

Whistle Stop Café Mysteries

Join best friends Debbie Albright and Janet Shaw as they step out in faith to open the Whistle Stop Café inside the historic train depot in Dennison, Ohio. During WWII, the depot's canteen workers offered doughnuts, sandwiches, and a heap of gratitude to thousands of soldiers on their way to war via troop-transport trains. Our sleuths soon find themselves on track to solve baffling mysteries—both past and present. Come along for the ride for stories of honor, duty to God and country, and of course fun, family, and friends!

Under the Apple Tree
As Time Goes By
We'll Meet Again
Till Then
I'll Be Seeing You
Fools Rush In
Let It Snow
Accentuate the Positive
For Sentimental Reasons

MYSTERIES OF BLACKBERRY VALLEY

That's My Baby
A String of Pearls
Somewhere Over the Rainbow
Down Forget-Me-Not Lane
Set the World on Fire
When You Wish Upon a Star
Rumors Are Flying
Here We Go Again
Stairway to the Stars
Winter Weather
Wait Till the Sun Shines
Now You're in My Arms
Sooner or Later
Apple Blossom Time
My Dreams Are Getting Better

Secrets from Grandma's Attic

Life is recorded not only in decades or years, but in events and memories that form the fabric of our being. Follow Tracy Doyle, Amy Allen, and Robin Davisson, the granddaughters of the recently deceased centenarian, Pearl Allen, as they explore the treasures found in the attic of Grandma Pearl's Victorian home, nestled near the banks of the Mississippi in Canton, Missouri. Not only do Pearl's descendants uncover a long-buried mystery at every attic exploration, they also discover their grandmother's legacy of deep, abiding faith, which has shaped and guided their family through the years. These uncovered Secrets from Grandma's Attic reveal stories of faith, redemption, and second chances that capture your heart long after you turn the last page.

History Lost and Found
The Art of Deception
Testament to a Patriot
Buttoned Up
Pearl of Great Price
Hidden Riches
Movers and Shakers
The Eye of the Cat
Refined by Fire

MYSTERIES OF BLACKBERRY VALLEY

The Prince and the Popper
Something Shady
Duel Threat
A Royal Tea
The Heart of a Hero
Fractured Beauty
A Shadowy Past
In Its Time
Nothing Gold Can Stay
The Cameo Clue
Veiled Intentions
Turn Back the Dial
A Marathon of Kindness
A Thief in the Night
Coming Home

Savannah Secrets

Welcome to Savannah, Georgia, a picture-perfect Southern city known for its manicured parks, moss-covered oaks, and antebellum architecture. Walk down one of the cobblestone streets, and you'll come upon Magnolia Investigations. It is here where two friends have joined forces to unravel some of Savannah's deepest secrets. Tag along as clues are exposed, red herrings discarded, and thrilling surprises revealed. Find inspiration in the special bond between Meredith Bellefontaine and Julia Foley. Cheer the friends on as they listen to their hearts and rely on their faith to solve each new case that comes their way.

The Hidden Gate
A Fallen Petal
Double Trouble
Whispering Bells
Where Time Stood Still
The Weight of Years
Willful Transgressions
Season's Meetings
Southern Fried Secrets
The Greatest of These
Patterns of Deception

MYSTERIES OF BLACKBERRY VALLEY

The Waving Girl
Beneath a Dragon Moon
Garden Variety Crimes
Meant for Good
A Bone to Pick
Honeybees & Legacies
True Grits
Sapphire Secret
Jingle Bell Heist
Buried Secrets
A Puzzle of Pearls
Facing the Facts
Resurrecting Trouble
Forever and a Day

Mysteries of Martha's Vineyard

Priscilla Latham Grant has inherited a lighthouse! So with not much more than a strong will and a sore heart, the recent widow says goodbye to her lifelong Kansas home and heads to the quaint and historic island of Martha's Vineyard, Massachusetts. There, she comes face-to-face with adventures, which include her trusty canine friend, Jake, three delightful cousins she didn't know she had, and Gerald O'Bannon, a handsome Coast Guard captain—plus head-scratching mysteries that crop up with surprising regularity.

A Light in the Darkness
Like a Fish Out of Water
Adrift
Maiden of the Mist
Making Waves
Don't Rock the Boat
A Port in the Storm
Thicker Than Water
Swept Away
Bridge Over Troubled Waters
Smoke on the Water
Shifting Sands
Shark Bait

MYSTERIES OF BLACKBERRY VALLEY

Seascape in Shadows
Storm Tide
Water Flows Uphill
Catch of the Day
Beyond the Sea
Wider Than an Ocean
Sheeps Passing in the Night
Sail Away Home
Waves of Doubt
Lifeline
Flotsam & Jetsam
Just Over the Horizon

A Note from the Editors

We hope you enjoyed another exciting volume in the Mysteries of Blackberry Valley series, published by Guideposts. For over seventy-five years, Guideposts, a nonprofit organization, has been driven by a vision of a world filled with hope. We aspire to be the voice of a trusted friend, a friend who makes you feel more hopeful and connected.

By making a purchase from Guideposts, you join our community in touching millions of lives, inspiring them to believe that all things are possible through faith, hope, and prayer. Your continued support allows us to provide uplifting resources to those in need. Whether through our communities, websites, apps, or publications, we inspire our audiences, bring them together, and comfort, uplift, entertain, and guide them. Visit us at guideposts.org to learn more.

We would love to hear from you. Write us at Guideposts, P.O. Box 5815, Harlan, Iowa 51593 or call us at (800) 932-2145. Did you love *Crooks and Christmas Cookies*? Leave a review for this product on guideposts.org/shop. Your feedback helps others in our community find relevant products.

Find inspiration, find faith, find Guideposts.

Shop our best sellers and favorites at
guideposts.org/shop

Or scan the QR code to go directly to our Shop

More Great Mysteries Are Waiting For Readers Like *You*!

Whistle Stop Café Mysteries

"Memories of a lifetime...I loved reading this story. Could not put the book down...." —ROSE H.

Mystery and WWII historical fiction fans will love these intriguing novels where two close friends piece together clues to solve mysteries past and present. Set in the real town of Dennison, Ohio, at a historic train depot where many soldiers once set off for war, these stories are filled with faithful, relatable characters you'll love spending time with.

Mysteries & Wonders of the Bible

"I so enjoyed this book....What a great insight into the life of the women who wove the veil for the Temple." —SHIRLEYN J.

Have you ever wondered what it might have been like to live back in Bible times to experience miraculous Bible events firsthand? Then you'll LOVE the fascinating **Mysteries & Wonders of the Bible** novels! Each Scripture-inspired story whisks you back to the ancient Holy Land, where you'll accompany ordinary men and women in their search for the hidden truths behind some of the most pivotal moments in the Bible. Each volume includes insights from a respected biblical scholar to help you ponder the significance of each story to your own life.

Mysteries of Cobble Hill Farm

"Wonderful series. Great story. Spellbinding. Could not put it down once I started reading." —BONNIE C.

Escape to the charming English countryside with **Mysteries of Cobble Hill Farm**, a heartwarming series of faith-filled mysteries. Harriet Bailey relocates to Yorkshire, England, to take over her late grandfather's veterinary practice, hoping it's the fresh start she needs. As she builds a new life, Harriet uncovers modern mysteries and long-buried secrets in the village and among the rolling hills and castle ruins. Each book is an inspiring puzzle where God's gentlest messengers—the animals in her care—help Harriet save the day.

Learn More & Shop These Exciting Mysteries, Biblical Stories, & Other Uplifting Fiction at **guideposts.org/fiction**